SpringerBriefs in Politic

For further volumes:
http://www.springer.com/series/8871

Alrik Thiem · Adrian Duşa

Qualitative Comparative Analysis with R

A User's Guide

 Springer

Alrik Thiem
Department of Humanities,
 Social and Political Sciences
Swiss Federal Institute of Technology
Zurich
Switzerland

Adrian Duşa
Department of Sociology
University of Bucharest
Bucharest
Romania

ISSN 2191-5466
ISBN 978-1-4614-4583-8
DOI 10.1007/978-1-4614-4584-5
Springer New York Heidelberg Dordrecht London

ISSN 2191-5474   (electronic)
ISBN 978-1-4614-4584-5   (eBook)

Library of Congress Control Number: 2012941421

Printed on acid-free paper

Springer is part of Springer Science+Business Media (www.springer.com)

For S.P. (soon S.T.)
and
A.R.M.

Preface

Over the past decade, Qualitative Comparative Analysis (QCA) has made major inroads into many areas of the social sciences, with applications from sociology and political science topping the list of publication figures. The development of software able to meet the growing demand for QCA, however, has been relatively slow and patchy. The QCA package for the R environment and this accompanying user's guide form the bundle of tools which fill this gap in three ways. First, with QCA, there now exists a user-friendly yet immensely powerful and flexible software solution covering the full spectrum of QCA. Second, this guide complements QCA's own internal documentation files by providing a comprehensive manual. And third, this guide offers a general introduction to performing QCA with the R environment for statistical computing and graphics.

The typographic conventions used in this book are intended to facilitate the flow of reading. Software and packages are identified by a sans-serif font: Software; R input code by slanted typewriter style: *input*; R output and general code by typewriter style: output; variables by italicized letters: *var*; sets (their negations) by bold upper case (lower case) font-weight: **S** (**s**); uniform resource locators (URLs) by typewriter style: http://www.r-project.org/; filename extensions by italicized lower case letters with a preceding dot: *.txt*; and explanations of R functions and some arguments by underlineation: sin() finds the sine.

Terminology is important and should ideally be homogeneous, but different academic communities use different terms to mean one and the same QCA object. We adopt a set of definitions that will be used consistently throughout the text. A *condition*, or *condition set* is a set, or a combination of sets, that is meant to explain the outcome. An *outcome*, or *outcome set* is a set that is to be explained by the condition(s). Each binary-value set has two *literals*, one for its presence and one for its absence/negation. An *outcome value* is a truth value in the truth table indicating the degree to which the aggregate evidence is consistent with the statement that the configuration is sufficient for the outcome. If the outcome value is positive ("1"), the configuration is assessed as *true*. If the outcome value is negative ("0"), the configuration is assessed as *false*. A *configuration* is a conjunctive combination of all conditions in the truth table. A *combination* is any conjunction or disjunction of conditions. The set of configurations which is to be minimized forms the *canonical sum*. A configuration which is part of a canonical sum is called a *fundamental product*. The *solution* results from the minimization of the canonical sum, and consists of one or more *minimal sums*. Each conjunctive combination in the minimal sum is called a *prime implicant*. Prime implicants that imply fundamental products which no other prime implicant implies are referred to as *essential prime implicants*, otherwise as *inessential prime implicants*.

When one of QCA's functions is introduced for the first time in a chapter, the full syntax is written out in a gray box as it would apply to the actual operation that is to be performed next. This not only presents readers with the full range of options they have available in this function, but also demonstrates the most efficient way to carry out the desired operation. For example, if the aim was to calibrate a crisp set S from a continuous base variable s, the following syntax box would appear before the actual input of code required by the user. The "is-greater-than" sign > indicates where the input of code starts, while the "plus" sign + signals the continuation of this input.

Full syntax:

```
> calibrate (s, type = "crisp", thresholds = 7, include = TRUE,
+  logistic = FALSE, idm = 0.95, ecdf = FALSE, p = 1, q = 1)
```

The above is the full syntax processed by QCA's `calibrate()` function, but only the following input is required by the user to achieve the desired result:

```
> S <- calibrate(s, thresholds = 7)
```

Often in the book we draw parallels and illustrate differences in the functionality between the QCA package and alternative software. Whenever mention is made of fs/QCA, QCA3, Tosmana or fuzzy, we refer to the latest versions available at the time of writing, this being fs/QCA 2.5, QCA3 0.0-5, Tosmana 1.3.2.0, and fuzzy st0140_2. Future updates may render these parallels and differences invalid.

The ideational spadework of this book was done during the 2011 Summer School of the European Consortium for Political Research (ECPR) at the University of Ljubljana, where I (Alrik) was lucky enough to meet a number of inspirational people. We thank Flavia Fossati for her help with the collection of QCA applications, and the participants of the 2012 ECPR Joint Sessions Workshop "Methodological Advances, Bridges and Limits in the Application of Qualitative Comparative Analysis" for useful comments and suggestions. Our editors at Springer Jon Gurstelle and Kevin Halligan ensured a smooth flow of this project. For financial support at various stages, we thank the Swiss Academy of Humanities and Social Sciences, the Swiss Study Foundation, and the Swiss National Science Foundation. This book has been typeset with the help of LATEX, BIBTEX, MakeIndex, PSTricks, and Sweave. Without these amazing tools, its preparation would have been so much harder. We also thank their authors for making such great software freely available.

A lot of time and effort has been invested in developing the **QCA** package and in writing this book. If you use the **QCA** package in your work, please cite it as

Duşa, Adrian, and Alrik Thiem. 2012. *QCA: Qualitative Comparative Analysis.* R Package Version <current version number>.

We seek to keep **QCA**'s functionality and design abreast of changes. Responsiveness to new developments and feedback by users are key in this endeavor. Readers of this book and users of our package are therefore invited to contact us with suggestions for improvements, comments, or questions at `thiem@sipo.gess.ethz.ch` and `dusadrian@unibuc.ro`.

Happy *QCA*ing!

Zurich, Switzerland, May 2012
Bucharest, Romania, May 2012

Alrik Thiem
Adrian Duşa

Contents

Abbreviations

CRAN	Comprehensive R Archive Network
CSA	Contradictory Simplifying Assumption
csQCA	crisp-set Qualitative Comparative Analysis
ECDF	Emprical Cumulative Distribution Function
fsQCA	fuzzy-set Qualitative Comparative Analysis
mvQCA	multi-value Qualitative Comparative Analysis
PI	Prime Implicant
POF	Parameters of Fit
PRI	Proportional Reduction in Inconsistency
QCA	Qualitative Comparative Analysis
SA	Simplifying Assumption
TOSMANA	Tool for Small-N Analysis
tQCA	temporal Qualitative Comparative Analysis

Chapter 1
Introduction

It is not an overstatement to say Qualitative Comparative Analysis (QCA) counts among the most influential innovations social science methodology has witnessed in the past two decades. The accomplishment of this status can be attributed almost exclusively to the untiring work of Charles Ragin. A political sociologist by trade, he has done more than anyone else for the recognition and diffusion of QCA. It then comes as no surprise that, although initially embraced only by a small number of macrosociologists (e.g., Amenta et al. 1992; Griffin et al. 1991; Ragin et al. 1984; Wickham-Crowley 1991), QCA has since made major inroads into political science (e.g., Avdagic 2010; Pennings 2003; Vis 2009; Werner 2009) and international relations (e.g., Chan 2003; Koenig-Archibugi 2004; Maat 2011; Thiem 2011). More recently, it has also been increasingly applied in business studies and economics (e.g., Abell 1990; Evans and Aligica 2008; Schneider et al. 2010; Valliere et al. 2008; Woodside et al. 2011), management and organization (e.g., Bakker et al. 2011; Boudet et al. 2011; Greckhamer 2011; Romme 1995), governance and administration (e.g., Kaeding 2008; Maggetti 2007; Stevenson and Greenberg 2000), legal studies and criminology (Arvind and Stirton 2010; Miethe and Drass 1999; Musheno et al. 1991; Williams and Farell 1990), education (e.g., Freitag and Schlicht 2009; Glaesser and Cooper 2011; Schneider and Sadowski 2010), health research (e.g., Blackman 2008; Harkreader and Imershein 1999; Hollingsworth et al. 1996; Schensul et al. 2010), environmental sciences (e.g., Oldekop et al. 2010; Rudel and Roper 1996; Scouvart et al. 2008), anthropology (e.g., Moritz et al. 2011), and religion (e.g., Sebastian and Parameswaran 2007). Publications which have sought to raise researchers' awareness of QCA have often preceded the proliferation of applications in many of these areas (Coverdill et al. 1994; Downey and Stanyer 2010; Greckhamer et al. 2008; Hellström 1998; Kitchener et al. 2002; Ragin 1989, 1999; Stokke 2007).

Figure 1.1 conveys a sense of QCA's trajectory by visualizing the trend in the total number of published journal article applications, broken down by its three related variants *crisp-set QCA* (csQCA), *multi-value QCA* (mvQCA) and *fuzzy-set QCA*

A. Thiem and A. Duşa, *Qualitative Comparative Analysis with R*,
SpringerBriefs in Political Science, DOI: 10.1007/978-1-4614-4584-5_1,
© The Author(s) 2013

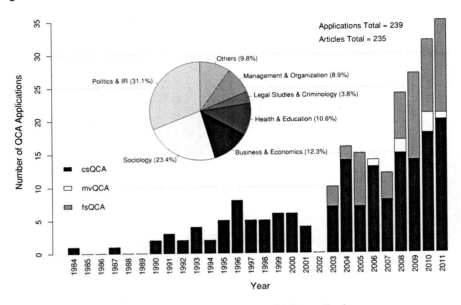

Fig. 1.1 Trend in number and research area distribution of QCA applications

(fsQCA).[1] It also shows the distribution of applications across areas of research. With the exception of the year 2002, there have been at least two in each year since 1990. After the appearance of Ragin's award-winning "The Comparative Method" (1987) and the introduction of csQCA, about four applications on average have been published in the years between 1990 and 2000, but only his "Fuzzy-Set Social Science" (2000) seems to have got the "Ragin Revolution" (Vaisey 2009) finally off ground. Allowing for a publication lag of about 2 years, the average number of applications rose to 13 in the years between 2003 and 2007. Since 2007, it almost tripled from 12 to 35 in 2011.

Despite the introduction of fsQCA, applications of csQCA have continued to increase from 7 in 2003 to 20 in 2011. As for fsQCA, they have increased from 3 in 2003 to 14 in 2011. In contrast to csQCA and fsQCA, however, mvQCA has remained at the sidelines so far. Of a total of 235 published articles between 1984 and 2011, only 7 have applied this QCA variant. Even when accounting for the fact

---

[1] The number of applications differs slightly from the number of articles as four articles have each presented two applications of QCA using two different variants. In order to be included in the data, articles had to focus primarily on a substantive research question, not QCA as a method or any of its constitutive procedures. In consequence, the number of published applications using or addressing QCA as a technique is probably between 20–30% higher. All entries are recorded in the bibliography section on http://www.compasss.org.

that mvQCA has only been introduced in 2004, 17 years after csQCA and 4 years after fsQCA, this represents an extremely low number.[2]

The distribution of publications across research areas reflects the background of QCA's earliest proponents. The vast majority of applications—close to 55%—have appeared in Sociology with 23% and Political Science, including International Relations, with 31%. Behind these two areas by large margins, approximately 12% have come from business and economics, 11% from health and education research, 9% from management and organization science, 4% from legal studies and criminology, and 10% from various other areas.

QCA's methodological success story has created a growing demand for tailored software, which has almost exclusively been met by two programs: Charles Ragin, Kriss Drass and Sean Davey's (2009) fs/QCA, and Lasse Cronqvist's (2011) Tosmana. Until very recently, however, neither program supported other operating systems than Microsoft Windows. As of version 1.3.2.0, Tosmana also runs on non-Windows operating systems. Kyle Longest and Stephen Vaisey's (2008) Stata package fuzzy and the R package QCA3 by Ronggui Huang (2012) have recently been offered as cross-platform alternatives.

All four of these software solutions offer various procedures, but none covers the full range of essential functionality. Neither fs/QCA nor fuzzy can handle multi-value data, while Tosmana cannot process fuzzy sets. An algorithm for arriving at intermediate solutions is only available in fs/QCA, and parameters of fit are not presented by Tosmana. In consequence, users have often been limited in their analyses when using one software, or had to switch back and fourth between different programs. Our book and the QCA package now form a comprehensive solution that not only unifies the individual capabilities of other software, but what is more, also enhances them further. Novel procedures include, among others, an automated search for necessary conditions and intermediate solutions for mvQCA.

R is an obvious choice of environment for this task because it is one of the most powerful tools for data analysis. Popular with natural as well as mathematically inclined social scientists for its almost unrivaled flexibility, however, R comes at the price of a steep learning curve. As Chambers (2008, 34) puts it, the "computational style of an R session is extremely general", and "for some users exactly this computational style and diversity present barriers to using the system". With the combination of a new R package for performing QCA and a book that accompanies it, we thus pursue two main objectives: first, to draw on the tremendous capabilities of R in order to meet the demand for software that is capable of performing the entire range of QCA procedures on all operating systems, and second, to lower the barriers which have thus far ruled out R for many users of QCA as an alternative software environment.

This book therefore starts with a brief introduction to R, which we have kept to the absolute minimum necessary to perform QCA with the QCA package. If the reader's intention is to carry on with R beyond this text, we highly recommend a

---

[2] We doubt that this is a consequence of the rare use of multi-nominal variables in social-science research.

more thorough introductory exposure to R. Due to its ever increasing popularity also among social scientists, the number of elementary, intermediate, and advanced textbooks on R in general and on specific topics in particular has kept growing. The R project website `http://www.r-project.org/` offers an extensive overview of available books, of which there have been 115 at the time of writing. In our view, one of the best general introductions to R for (complete) beginners is Zuur et al. (2009). A very good online source is offered by the Academic Technology Services of the University of California in Los Angeles (UCLA) at `http://www.ats.ucla.edu/stat/r/`.

No knowledge of R is assumed, but readers should be familiar with the fundamentals of Qualitative Comparative Analysis (QCA) as introduced by Ragin (1987, 2000, 2008) and Rihoux and Ragin (2009). Many core concepts are revisited in brief at the beginning of a section or in a footnote, but the focus of our text is on combining prior knowledge of QCA with almost no or little knowledge of R. Where methodologically novel concepts or procedures appear, we explain them in sufficient theoretical detail prior to demonstrating their implementation in QCA.

Chapter 3 on csQCA and Chap. 4 on fsQCA are self-contained because researchers still think of these two variants as related yet distinct techniques. This is justified to the degree that some procedures are relevant for one, but not the other variant. For example, Venn diagrams are inappropriate for fsQCA. While this approach leads to some duplication of code and text, we consider it more user-friendly because time-consuming jumping back and forth between chapters and sections is avoided. In contrast, Chap. 5 on mvQCA and temporal QCA (tQCA) requires the reader to have studied at least Chap. 3.

The content of this book revolves around four main parts. First, we provide a concise introduction to the R environment for those readers with no or very little knowledge of the software. Although this introduction is kept to an absolute minimum, it contains all necessary procedures required to perform QCA in R. Second, we show how to perform csQCA by replicating Krook's (2010) study on women's representation in Western national parliaments. The results from Emmenegger's (2011) fsQCA study on job-security regulations in Western democracies are replicated in the next chapter. Finally, a separate chapter on extensions of QCA introduces the procedures for mvQCA using Hartmann and Kemmerzell's (2010) study on party ban implementations in sub-Saharan Africa, and tQCA using the artificial dataset on student union recognitions at US research universities.

Chapter 2
Introduction to R

Abstract This chapter provides a brief introduction to the R environment. The material covers all topics that are necessary to understand the remaining chapters. In addition to basic arithmetic and logical operations, functions and values, data structures and functions that are fundamental to performing operations on sets and set memberships are introduced. Short sections on how to install R, text editors, and finding help complete the chapter.

2.1 Installation and Usage

If R is not yet installed, it should first be downloaded from the central R website at http://www.r-project.org. This website, shown in Fig. 2.1, provides information about R, its history, documentation, and other resources. In order to download the latest version of R, click on the *CRAN mirror* link in the *Getting Started* box.[1] Select a link under the country nearest to you and choose the appropriate version for your operating system. After the file has been downloaded, install the software with its default settings and open it.

First time users of R may be disappointed by what shows up: an unspectacular window similar to Fig. 2.2. However, R hides its light under the bushel, something you will discover over the course of this book. Most important at this stage is the R console inside the RGui window. The console provides information about the installed version and a few additional things. Unlike other statistical software such as SPSS, R possesses no integrated graphical user interface for communicating your commands to the software by means of radio buttons and mouse clicks.[2] Instead, the commands which tell the software what to do exactly have to be formulated using the

---

[1] CRAN stands for Comprehensive R Archive Network, describing all servers around the world on which code and documentation for R is stored.

[2] Some packages, such as the Rcmdr, add a graphical user interface.

A. Thiem and A. Duşa, *Qualitative Comparative Analysis with R*,
SpringerBriefs in Political Science, DOI: 10.1007/978-1-4614-4584-5_2,
© The Author(s) 2013

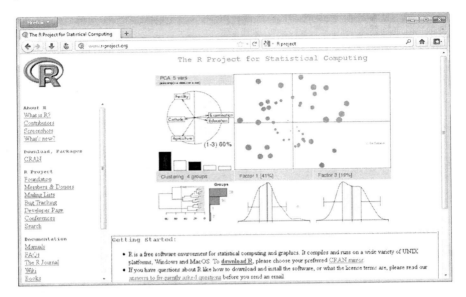

Fig. 2.1 The R website

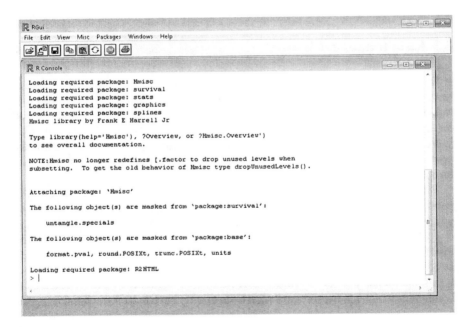

Fig. 2.2 Starting a session in R

language of R. It expects these commands in the console where the blinking cursor appears next to the "is-greater-than" sign >.

2.2 Installing and Loading Packages

A package is a directory system containing R code, documentation, and sometimes also data. Packages extend the software by making functions which are not part of the basic distribution available to the user. Some essential packages are already included by default, but the vast majority of packages has to be installed separately.[3] For example, the QCA package contains functions for performing QCA, but it also contains datasets and help files which document everything. Packages which do not come as part of the basic R distribution can be installed through the RGui menu (*Packages→Install package(s)...*) or the `install.packages()` function. Type the following code into the console and press the [Enter] key. This will install the QCA package.

```
> install.packages("QCA", dependencies = TRUE)
```

The `dependencies` argument is set to TRUE, which causes all other packages on which the functionality of the QCA package depends to also be installed. The QCA package incorporates functionality provided in the lpSolve package, so lpSolve will be installed alongside QCA. The mere installation of a package, however, is not enough to make its functionality available. Packages also have to be loaded into R at the beginning of a session, either through the RGui menu (*Packages→Load package...*) or the `library()` command.

```
> library("QCA")
```

Installed packages should be regularly updated either through the menu (*Packages→Update packages...*) or the `update.packages()` function.

2.3 Basic Operations, Functions and Values

In essence, R can be conceived of as a programmable calculator whose core functionality can be extended almost limitlessly. Start by entering the following code in the console.

```
> 3 * 5

[1] 15
```

It does not matter whether spaces are left between the single elements. The two expressions 3*5 and 3 *5 yield the same result, but once expressions become more complex, leaving sensible, and avoiding unnecessary, blank spaces

---

[3] At the time of writing, about 3,900 packages have been available on CRAN.

in a structured manner is highly advisable. The [1] in front of the result is called the *index*. We will come back to what indexes are useful for at a later stage. This minimal example already illustrates the basic work flow in R: first formulate a command and then send it to the interpreter for processing.

R is an object-oriented language, which means that everything is treated as an object, including functions. A function f has the following structure in R:

```
> f(argument1 = value1, argument2 = value2, ...)
```

For example, the <u>sin</u>e function is implemented in R as sin().[4]

```
> sin(pi/2)

[1] 1
```

There are many other such basic functions. For example, instead of using the * operator for calculating the product of 3 and 5, the prod() function could have been invoked.

```
> prod(3, 5)

[1] 15
```

Besides standard names for specific functions, R also has a standard notation for certain values, such as pi for π, NA for missing data, and NULL for empty sets. If an operation is performed which is not defined, R returns NaN (<u>n</u>ot <u>a n</u>umber). Note that the division of zero by zero returns NaN, whereas the division of a nonzero number by zero returns Inf, which designates <u>inf</u>inity.

```
> 0/0

[1] NaN

> 1/0

[1] Inf
```

In addition to these arithmetic objects, R also offers logical operators, functions, and values. The two logical values are TRUE (true) and FALSE (false). Logical functions include == (is equal) and != (is not equal).

```
> 6 == 7

[1] FALSE

> 6 != 7

[1] TRUE
```

---

[4] The sine of an angle is the ratio of the length of the side opposite of this angle in a right-angled triangle to the length of the longest side.

Table 2.1 Basic operators, functions, and values

Operator / Function / Value		Description
Arithmetic	+, −	Addition, subtraction
	*, /	Multiplication, division
	^	Power
Logical	&, &&	And, and (not vector-valued)
	|, ||	Or, or (not vector-valued)
	xor	Either … or
Arithmetic	sum(), prod()	Sum, product
	min(), max()	Minimum, maximum
	round(), floor(), ceiling()	Round (down / up to integer)
	sqrt()	Square root
	abs()	Modulus
	log()	Natural logarithm
	exp()	Exponential function
Logical	==, !=	Equals, equals not
	>, >=	Larger, larger or equal
	<, <=	Smaller, smaller or equal
	!	Not (negation)
Arithmetic	pi	π
	Inf, -Inf	Positive and negative infinity
	NA	Missing value
	NULL	Empty set
	NaN	Not a number
Logical	TRUE, FALSE	True, false

Two important logical operators are & (and), and | (or).

```
> FALSE & TRUE
```

```
[1] FALSE
```

```
> 2 == 2 | 2 == 3
```

```
[1] TRUE
```

A summary of basic operators, functions, and values available in R, both arithmetic and logical, is given in Table 2.1. We leave it to the reader to experiment with those that have not been introduced in this section.

2.4 Using an Editor

It is inefficient to type commands into the console. Once code grows to more than simple one-line calculations, a good editor becomes an indispensable tool. Editors also aid in identifying programming errors, they ease commenting and sometimes

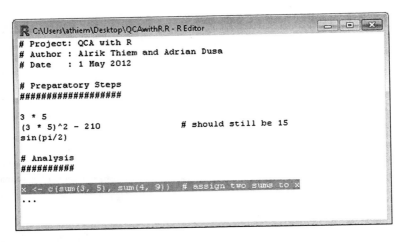

Fig. 2.3 The R script editor

even provide built-in function templates. On the MacOS and Windows operating systems, R comes with a basic editor. It can be started in the RGui window via the menu entry *File→New script*. This rudimentary editor suffices for everything that is presented in this book, but if you intend to carry on with R and the QCA package, we strongly recommend the use of a more sophisticated editor. A good overview of what is available can be found at `http://www.sciviews.org/_rgui/projects/Editors.html`.

In order to send commands from the R editor to the console, type the command without preceding it by the "is-greater-than" sign >, mark it (with or without comments) and press [Ctrl + R] as shown in Fig. 2.3. The marked code will be send to the console and executed. At the end of a session, scripts can be saved as *.R* files through the editor menu *File→Save as....*

Besides a good editor, larger projects should also make use of comments, which provide information relating to the code. Comments not only make it easier to keep track of code or re-use it in other projects, but they also allow peers to better understand and replicate results. As replication is a cornerstone of scientific research, the practice of commenting is not to be underestimated. In R, comments can be inserted with the "hash" sign #, after which everything else on the same line will be ignored.

```
> (3 * 5)^2 - 210     # should still be 15

[1] 15
```

2.5   Objects and Assignments

It was mentioned above that R is an object-oriented language. Object-orientation not only means that functions are treated as objects, but also that results from operations using these functions can themselves be saved as objects again. This process is referred to as *assignment*. The most common form of assignment uses the *assignment arrow*, which consists of the "is smaller than" sign < and the "minus" sign – joined together, without spaces in between.

```
> x <- c(sum(3, 5), sum(4, 9)) # assigning two sums to x
```

The two built-in functions c() and sum() have been used here to arrive at a result that is then assigned to the new object x.[5] The c() function concatenates its arguments, the two sums of $3 + 5 = 8$ and $4 + 9 = 13$.[6] In order to avoid mistakes, a new object should thus not be named with the lower case letter c. As R is case-sensitive, upper case C would have also been fine. More generally, however, a name of an object should be an optimal trade-off between a description of its content and efficient programming. For example, one way of naming is to combine lower and upper case letters, as in dataAuthor for a dataset. This way of naming is referred to as *camel notation*. Another system uses a dot as the separator, as in data.author. When x is now entered, the result of the expression assigned to it is called up and printed into the console.

```
> x
```

```
[1]   8 13
```

As expected, x consists of two elements—the two sums of 8 and 13—which are preceded by the index [1]. R only shows the index of the first element in that line of the console. To see what happens beyond the first line, enter the following code, including the enclosing parentheses. If necessary, resize the console window.

```
> (x <- rep(5, times = 40))
```

```
[1] 5 5 5 5 5 5 5 5 5 5 5 5 5 5 5 5 5 5 5 5 5 5 5 5 5
[26] 5 5 5 5 5 5 5 5 5 5 5 5 5 5 5
```

A new object x has been created by overwriting the original one that consisted of two sums. This new object results from the rep() function, which repeats its first argument as often as specified in its second argument times. Now the indexing extends over several lines, with only the index of the first element in that line being displayed. Putting parentheses around an entire expression is a useful shortcut to calling up the object by retyping its name.

---

[5] The sum() function was listed in Table 2.1 above. It adds together all its arguments.

[6] Typing 3 + 5 is an alternative to sum(3, 5).

2.6 Data Structures

A *data structure* is a particular form of arrangement which usually represents the nature of the elements it consists of. A number of different data structures exist in R, but this section focuses on those which occur most often in social science research—*vectors*, *matrices*, *data frames*, and *lists*.

2.6.1 Vectors

Vectors generally represent single rows or columns of data. A single number is also a vector, but a special type thereof referred to as a *scalar*. You have already created two vectors, one of length two and the other of length fifty, using the c() and the rep() functions in Sect. 2.5. The length of a vector is the number of elements it comprises. It can be found with the length() function.

```
> x <- rep(5, times = 50)
> length(x)

[1] 50
```

Vectors need not necessarily consist of numbers. For example, the three words "Qualitative", "Comparative", and "Analysis" can be concatenated to form a single vector of length three.

```
> (y <- c("Qualitative", "Comparative", "Analysis"))

[1] "Qualitative" "Comparative" "Analysis"
```

Besides the c() and the rep() functions, the seq() function is also often used to generate vectors which have some sequential structure.

```
> seq(from = 0, to = 10, by = 2)

[1]  0  2  4  6  8 10
```

The first two arguments from and to indicate the sequence starting and end points, while by specifies the increment. If the starting point and the increment are to equal one, then a shorter route can be taken.

```
> seq(10)

 [1]  1  2  3  4  5  6  7  8  9  10
```

Sequences of increment one that consist only of integers can be easily produced using a colon.

```
> 1:5

[1] 1 2 3 4 5
```

2.6.2 Matrices

A matrix is a rectangular arrangement of elements on which mathematical operations can be performed. The `matrix()` function offers the easiest way to create matrices in R.

```
> x <- seq(20)
> matrix(x, nrow = 5)

     [,1] [,2] [,3] [,4]
[1,]    1    6   11   16
[2,]    2    7   12   17
[3,]    3    8   13   18
[4,]    4    9   14   19
[5,]    5   10   15   20
```

In addition to the first argument x representing the data, the function can take two further arguments: `nrow` for the number of rows and `ncol` for the number of columns. It suffices to provide either the former or the latter. Matrices are filled column-wise by default. For row-wise filling the argument `byrow = TRUE` should be used.

Matrices can also be constructed from existing row or column vectors. The `cbind()` function binds columns together, whereas the `rbind()` function binds rows together.

```
> x <- rep(seq(4), 2)
> y <- rep(c(7, 8), 4)
> rbind(x, y)

  [,1] [,2] [,3] [,4] [,5] [,6] [,7] [,8]
x    1    2    3    4    1    2    3    4
y    7    8    7    8    7    8    7    8
```

Notice that the name for the second argument in the `rep()` function—`times`—has been omitted. The `rep()` function "knows" that the second argument is always the number of times the first argument should be repeated. The omission of argument names works for all R functions, but for didactic reasons, we will always write them out.

A peculiar feature of R can be nicely demonstrated with matrices—vector recycling. It allows to perform operations and create objects which are usually mathematically impossible. Enter the following block of code, the two last input lines of which seem meaningless.

```
> x <- seq(4)
> y <- rep(c(7, 8), 4)
> rbind(x, y)
```

```
     [,1] [,2] [,3] [,4] [,5] [,6] [,7] [,8]
x     1    2    3    4    1    2    3    4
y     7    8    7    8    7    8    7    8

> x + y

[1]  8 10 10 12  8 10 10 12
```

It remains true that two vectors of different lengths cannot be bound together to create a matrix. Vector x is of length four, y of length eight. Also, vector addition is undefined for summands of unequal length. In these and similar cases, however, R automatically recycles the shorter vector as long as the length of the longer vector is a multiple of the length of the shorter vector.

2.6.3 Data Frames

Data frames are the most common data structure in the social sciences. They are very similar to matrices, but unlike matrices, which can only contain data of one *data type*, data frames can accommodate different types. Let us first create a small data frame from the information about the three QCA variants that was presented in the introduction in Fig. 1.1 using the data.frame() function.

```
> QCAdat <- data.frame(variant = c("csQCA", "mvQCA", "fsQCA"),
+   number = c(170, 7, 62))
> QCAdat

  variant number
1   csQCA    170
2   mvQCA      7
3   fsQCA     62
```

The data frame consists of three rows and two columns. The particularity of QCAdat is that the first column contains elements which consist only of letters, whereas the second column's elements are numbers. The two columns therefore contain data of different data types.

2.6.4 Lists

Data frames are special cases of *lists*, another useful data structure in R. Lists are extremely flexible because they can store all of the above structures in a single object. The creation of lists is achieved with the list() function.

Table 2.2 Basic data types

Type	Description		Example
Logical	Logical values		TRUE
Numeric	Real numbers	*Integer*	3
		Double	2.71
Character	Letters and strings		"QCA"

```
> (QCAlist <- list(dat = QCAdat, txt = c("Happy", "QCAing")))

$dat
  variant number
1   csQCA    170
2   mvQCA      7
3   fsQCA     62

$txt
[1] "Happy"  "QCAing"
```

Rarely are lists created directly by end-users. Instead, they are usually generated when a complex function, such as **QCA**'s `truthTable()`, returns a result that is not just a single number, but a collection of several different objects.

2.7 Data Types

At the most basic level, objects can be divided into different atomic *data types*. Three such types are listed in Table 2.2 in increasing order of hierarchy. The lowest priority is given to *logical*, the highest to *character* values. *Numeric* values fall in between. The reason for this hierarchy builds on set relations. It is possible to represent all real numbers with character strings, but not the other way around. It will later be shown that real numbers can in turn represent the logical values TRUE and FALSE, but logical values cannot represent all real numbers. In set-theoretic language, the set of logical values is a subset of the set of real numbers, which is itself a subset of the set of character values. The real numbers are further divided into *integer* and *double*, the former of which is again a subset of the latter.[7]

Below we define two vectors, the first consisting of three letters, the second of a sequence of six numbers.[8]

---

[7] More precisely, *numeric* is identical to *double*.

[8] The two objects `letters` and `LETTERS` are predefined constants in R.

```
> (Letters <- c("Q", "C", "A"))

[1] "Q" "C" "A"

> (Numbers <- seq(from = 1, to = 2, by = 0.2))

[1] 1.0 1.2 1.4 1.6 1.8 2.0
```

The data type of `Letters` and `Numbers` can be queried with the `mode()` function.

```
> mode(Letters)

[1] "character"

> mode(Numbers)

[1] "numeric"
```

The data type of `Letters` is *character*, that of `Numbers` is *numeric*. The two are now to be concatenated with the `c()` function to create the new object `LetNum`. The data type of `LetNum` will be *character*, not *numeric*, because that data type which is highest in the hierarchy will always be chosen so as to avoid a loss of information.

```
> (LetNum <- c(Letters, Numbers))

[1] "Q"   "C"   "A"   "1"   "1.2" "1.4" "1.6" "1.8" "2"

> mode(LetNum)

[1] "character"
```

Whether or not an object is of a specific data type can be tested with the function class `is.<data type>()`.

```
> is.character(Letters)

[1] TRUE
```

While `is.<data type>()` only tests for the data type, the function class `as.<data type>()` can be used in order to coerce objects to specific data types.

```
> (Numbers <- as.integer(Numbers))

[1] 1 1 1 1 1 2
```

The vector `Numbers` remains *numeric*, but it is now not *double* anymore.[9]

---

[9] Note that `as.integer()` works similarly to the `floor()` function presented in Table 2.1.

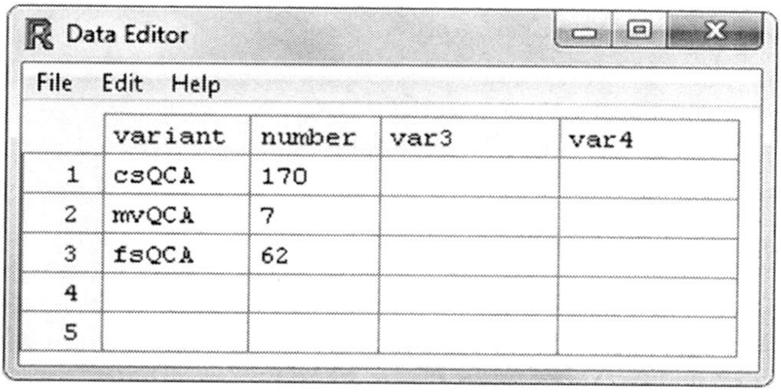

Fig. 2.4 R data editor

2.8 Accessing Data

Working with and operating on datasets in R is different from working with general spreadsheet software. We introduce several ways of accessing data in this section, each of which may be more useful than the other in certain situations. As a preparatory step, let us recreate the data frame QCAdat from Sect. 2.6.3, which gave the number of times each QCA variant has been applied.

```
> QCAdat <- data.frame(variant = c("csQCA", "mvQCA", "fsQCA"),
+   number = c(170, 7, 62))
> QCAdat

  variant number
1   csQCA    170
2   mvQCA      7
3   fsQCA     62
```

The data frame can be seen in the R console, but trying to change elements in QCAdat from within the console will not work. There exist several ways whereby QCAdat can be accessed. For example, the edit() function can be used for small changes, such as the replacement of single values or a correction of a variable label. It will call up the built-in R data editor shown in Fig. 2.4.

```
> QCAdat <- edit(QCAdat)
```

The data frame is conveniently small, but problems arise if, for example, a new variable with the recoded values of an existing variable in a larger dataset should be added. For this and similar purposes, the "dollar" sign $ is useful. Suppose a nominally-scaled variable indicating in which research area the occurrence of each QCA variant has been highest should be generated. Applications of csQCA have appeared most often in sociology, those of mvQCA and fsQCA in political science.

```
> QCAdat$occur <- c("sociology", rep("politics", 2))
> QCAdat
```

```
  variant number    occur
1   csQCA   170 sociology
2   mvQCA     7  politics
3   fsQCA    62  politics
```

The variable *occur* is created within QCAdat by putting a $ in front of it. As both mvQCA and fsQCA applications have occurred most often in political science, the rep() function avoids typing in the character value "politics" twice. The $ sign can also be applied to perform operations on existing variables. For computing the total number of QCA applications, the sum() function can be run over all values in the respective column.

```
> sum(QCAdat$number)
```

```
[1] 239
```

Sometimes access to only a subset of the data may be needed. Possibly more than a few values of a variable but fewer than all of them. In such cases, the subset() function is useful.

```
> subset(QCAdat, subset = number > 50)
```

```
  variant number    occur
1   csQCA   170 sociology
3   fsQCA    62  politics
```

Its argument subset requires a logical expression for the selection of elements or rows. A second argument of subset() is select, which specifies the desired columns.

```
> subset(QCAdat, select = variant)
```

```
  variant
1   csQCA
2   mvQCA
3   fsQCA
```

These two arguments can also be applied together in order to extract any combination of elements or rows and columns from the data.

```
> subset(QCAdat, subset = number > 50, select = variant)
```

```
  variant
1   csQCA
3   fsQCA
```

Another way of accessing data is through *indexing*, also referred to as *subscripting*. The structure of an index is `<object>[<row(s)>, <column(s)>]`. For example, in order to select the entry for the number of mvQCA applications, the second row has to be specified, because mvQCA applications are listed there, and the second column, because this is the variable with the number of applications.

```
> QCAdat[2, 2]
```

```
[1] 7
```

Now suppose all values from the number of applications should be extracted. In this case, a substitute for `QCAdat$number` is to leave away the row index and only provide the column index.

```
> QCAdat[ , 2]
```

```
[1] 170    7   62
```

It is also possible to use logical expressions, as in the `subset()` function, with indexes.

```
> QCAdat[QCAdat$number > 50, 2]
```

```
[1] 170   62
```

In the case of lists, a special way of indexing must be used. For example, in order to access the second element of the list object `QCAlist` created in Sect. 2.6.4, the value 2 should be enclosed by double square brackets.

```
> QCAlist[[2]]
```

```
[1] "Happy"   "QCAing"
```

After this more general introduction, the next two sections will now introduce useful functions for operating on the elements of sets and their set memberships.

2.9 Operations on Sets

This section introduces the basic operations available in R with regard to the elements of sets, not their membership, which is assumed to be crisp. Let us first create two equally-sized sets, **X** and **Y**, whose six elements are random samples of integers between one and ten.

```
> set.seed(1)
> (X <- sample(1:10, size = 6))
```

```
[1] 3 4 5 7 2 8
```

```
> set.seed(10)
> (Y <- sample(1:10, size = 6))
```

```
[1] 6 3 4 5 1 2
```

The set.seed() function is very useful whenever random sampling is applied because it allows the retrieval of the exact same sample. Its single argument is just a starting number for the random number generator. The sample() function takes a sample of the specified size from the elements of its first argument. The union of these two sets containing all *unique* elements which belong either to **X** or **Y** can be found with the union() function.

```
> union(X, Y)
```

```
[1] 3 4 5 7 2 8 6 1
```

In contrast, the intersection containing all unique elements which belong to **X** and **Y** can be found with the intersect() function.

```
> intersect(X, Y)
```

```
[1] 3 4 5 2
```

Another useful function is setdiff(), which returns all unique elements of the first set which are not unique elements of the second set.

```
> setdiff(X, Y)
```

```
[1] 7 8
```

The last function to be introduced is setequal(), which returns a logical statement about the equality between all *unique* elements of two sets.

```
> setequal(X, Y)
```

```
[1] FALSE
```

It is important to emphasize the word *unique* here, otherwise the result of the following example would be surprising.

```
> A <- c(1, 2, 3, 4)
> B <- c(1, 1, 2, 3, 3, 3, 4)
> setequal(A, B)
```

```
[1] TRUE
```

In this case, the test result is true because all unique elements in **A** and **B** are equal. However, if *exact* equality is to be tested, the identical() function should be used.

```
> B <- A
> identical(A, B)
```

```
[1] TRUE
```

2.10 Operations on Set Memberships

After basic operations on sets have been introduced, this section now demonstrates how to perform calculations on elements' set memberships. The two functions pmin() and pmax() are central for this purpose. Let us begin with a small dataset of fuzzy-set membership scores, named datFS. All functions and structures work exactly the same for crisp sets.

```
> set.seed(1)
> datFS <- data.frame(A = runif(5), B = runif(5), C = runif(5))
> (datFS <- round(datFS, 2))

    A    B    C
1 0.27 0.90 0.21
2 0.37 0.94 0.18
3 0.57 0.66 0.69
4 0.91 0.63 0.38
5 0.20 0.06 0.77
```

The dataset datFS consists of five cases with set membership scores in three conditions **A**, **B**, and **C**. The runif() function generates a random deviate from a uniform distribution for each case and condition. Before calling up datFS, the round() function introduced in Table 2.1 cuts these deviates back to two decimal places. Having created the dataset of set membership scores, the pmin() function can now be applied in order to calculate the result of the expression $\mathbf{a} \cdot \mathbf{B} \cdot \mathbf{C}$ (not **A** AND **B** AND **C**). The pmin() function returns parallel minima, which means that instead of simply taking the single smallest value from all values in the sets passed to pmin() as arguments, set membership scores are compared separately for each case (row). The computation of complements can be achieved by making use of the fact that for every set complement **set**, **set** $= 1 - \mathbf{SET}$.

```
> (datFS$aBC <- pmin(1 - datFS$A, datFS$B, datFS$C))

[1] 0.21 0.18 0.43 0.09 0.06
```

Recall that R recycles the value(s) of the shorter vector when performing operations on two vectors of different lengths. This is why the scalar 1 need not be repeated five times in order to compute the complement of **A**. The function pmax() is applied analogously for parallel maxima. For example, the result of the expression $\mathbf{A} + \mathbf{b} + \mathbf{C}$ (**A** OR not **B** OR **C**) can be calculated as follows:

```
> (datFS$"A+b+C" <- pmax(datFS$A, 1 - datFS$B, datFS$C))

[1] 0.27 0.37 0.69 0.91 0.94
```

The set name for the new disjunctive combination has to be enclosed in double quotes because the Boolean "or" sign + would otherwise be treated as an arithmetic operator rather than part of a string. The two functions pmin() and pmax() can also be combined in nested structures so that even complex expressions require relatively little programming effort. As an example, let us calculate $\mathbf{A} \cdot \mathbf{b} + \mathbf{B} \cdot \mathbf{c}$.

```
> datFS$"Ab+Bc" <- pmax(
+  pmin(datFS$A, 1 - datFS$B),
+  pmin(datFS$B, 1 - datFS$C)
+ )
> datFS
```

```
      A    B    C  aBC A+b+C Ab+Bc
1  0.27 0.90 0.21 0.21  0.27  0.79
2  0.37 0.94 0.18 0.18  0.37  0.82
3  0.57 0.66 0.69 0.43  0.69  0.34
4  0.91 0.63 0.38 0.09  0.91  0.62
5  0.20 0.06 0.77 0.06  0.94  0.20
```

Even complete truth tables can be constructed with pmin() and pmax(). Instead of using numeric truth values of 1 and 0, here we choose TRUE and FALSE in order to demonstrate why, as stated in Sect. 2.7, these logical values are subsets of real numbers in R. Using QCA's createMatrix() function, enter the following code to construct the first part of the truth table tt, containing all 2^k configurations from the $k = 3$ crisp sets $\mathbf{A}$, $\mathbf{B}$, and $\mathbf{C}$.[10]

```
> tt <- data.frame(createMatrix(rep(2, 3), logical = TRUE))
> names(tt) <- c("A", "B", "C")
```

After having generated all $2^3 = 8$ configurations, the condition labels for sets $\mathbf{A}$, $\mathbf{B}$, and $\mathbf{C}$ are assigned to each column of tt using the names() function. The outcome value (truth value) of the expression $\mathbf{a} \cdot \mathbf{B} \cdot \mathbf{C}$ can then be computed as follows:

```
> tt$OUT <- pmin(1 - tt$A, tt$B, tt$C)
> tt
```

```
      A     B     C OUT
1 FALSE FALSE FALSE   0
2 FALSE FALSE  TRUE   0
3 FALSE  TRUE FALSE   0
4 FALSE  TRUE  TRUE   1
5  TRUE FALSE FALSE   0
6  TRUE FALSE  TRUE   0
7  TRUE  TRUE FALSE   0
8  TRUE  TRUE  TRUE   0
```

---

[10] The createMatrix() function is primarily used internally for constructing truth tables.

In R, the logical value TRUE is equivalent to the numerical value 1, whereas FALSE corresponds to the numerical value 0. The set of logical values is therefore a subset of the set of real numbers and R can calculate the result of 1 - FALSE. In consequence, the only true statement in the truth table tt for the expression **a · B · C** is the combination FALSE-TRUE-TRUE in row four.

2.11 Importing and Exporting Data

Social-science datasets are rarely built directly in R, but usually in spreadsheet or database software such as Excel or Access. It is thus important to know how to import external data files. R can read many different file formats and from different sources, but the easiest way is to first prepare the data in a spreadsheet software and save it as a tab-delimited text file.[11] This file type ensures a small file size and it can be easily imported into all kinds of software on all kinds of operating systems. Make sure that no cell entry, including values, row, and column labels, has a blank space. Blank spaces should generally be avoided, irrespective of whether the data is to be further analyzed in another software or not. Instead of naming a variable *GDP Growth*, *GDPgrowth* should be used. In addition, all entries or empty cells denoting missing values should already be marked with NA.[12]

In the bibliography section at http://www.compasss.org a number of datasets from published studies can be found. Download one of them and save it in the working directory of your R installation. The working directory is the folder from which R has been started. Its path can be found by entering the command getwd().

```
> getwd()
```

The working directory can be changed by providing a file path to the setwd() function.

```
> setwd("C:/Myfolder")
```

File path specifications use the following structure in R: "C:/.../..." or "C:\\...\\...". The familiar Microsoft Windows backslash structure "C:\...\..." cannot be used because the single backslash is a special character. Once the working directory has been found or changed to the preferred folder, and the dataset saved in it, the read.table() function will load it into the R workspace. The workspace is the working environment and includes all objects (vectors, matrices, data frames, functions, etc.) which have been created in the current session. For demonstration purposes, we use the dataset by Arvind and Stirton (2010) on the reception of the Code Napoleon in Germany.

---

[11] Text files have the file type extension *.txt*.

[12] R can handle other indicators for missing values, but an optimal preparation of the data according to R's standards facilitates their import.

```
> AS <- read.table("ArvindStirton2010set.txt", header = TRUE,
+  row.names = "State")
> AS
          D    C    F    I    L    N    A    O
Rhine 1.00 1.00 0.4 0.00 0.50 0.00 0.50 1.00
KiWes 1.00 0.75 0.6 0.00 0.60 0.00 0.90 1.00
GDBer 1.00 0.75 0.4 0.00 0.75 0.00 1.00 1.00
..... .... .... ... .... .... .... .... ....
<<rest omitted>>
```

The read.table() function makes AS a data frame by default. The original
file in which the data is stored is given as the first argument. By passing TRUE to
the optional header argument, the first row of ArvindStirton2010set.txt is
identified as containing the variable labels for AS. The name of the variable which
contains the case identifiers is passed to the row.names argument. If in your own
data the decimal separator is a comma instead of a point, dec = "," should be added
as an argument. If you neither want to save the data in your working directory nor
change the directory, the data can also be put into any folder and the entire file path
to R be provided instead.

Besides the read.table() function, there also exists a read.csv() function for
reading comma separated values. In addition, the foreign package provides functionality for importing data stored in other formats such as *.sav* (SPSS) or *.dta* (Stata).
We refer you to introductory textbooks on R and R's own manuals for further information on data import.

For saving data from R as *.txt* files, the write.table() function can be used.

```
> write.table(myfile, file = "myfile.txt", sep = "\t",
+  quote = FALSE)
```

The specification \t in the sep argument creates tab-separated values, and the
logical argument quote = FALSE avoids double quotes being put around character
values. This way, myfile will be structured in exactly the same way as the file
ArvindStirton2010set.txt.

2.12 Finding Help

Sometimes software lets you cry for help. If new to R, this will happen all the more
so. The learning curve for R is steep at the beginning, but once you have become
familiar with the fundamentals, the "products" it delivers will often have been cheap
at twice the price. However, even experienced users regularly seek help because
every new project will at least be a little different from the previous one and possibly
require a slightly different solution.

The first point of reference is R's internal help facilities, which can be accessed
with the question mark ?, followed by the term which is sought. This will open the

respective documentation files, in HTML or plain text format. For example, to look up the documentation for the prod() function, type the following:

```
> ?prod
```

Help pages have a standardized structure with all necessary information. Let us go through the most important headings, including *Description, Usage, Arguments, Details, Value,* and *Examples* because you will certainly come across them again. The *Description* states what the object you asked for is about. Not surprisingly, the prod() function returns the product. The *Usage* section shows the complete structure of prod(). Each element in this structure is explained under *Arguments*. The three dots . . . denote numeric or complex or logical vectors. Without going into the details here (the meaning of *numeric* and *logic* vectors has been explained in Sect. 2.7), this means that we could have also told R to calculate the product of 3 and 5, as we did above in Sect. 2.3 with the * operator, by passing to the prod() function the two numeric values 3 and 5.

```
> prod(3, 5)
```

```
[1] 15
```

The second element in the *Arguments* list is na.rm. This argument is logical, which implies that only one of two values can be passed to it: TRUE or FALSE. Under the *Usage* section, you saw that the default value of this argument was set to FALSE. It means that missing values in the vectors provided will not be removed unless specified otherwise by the user. This is very important! Compare the two following examples.

```
> x <- c(3, 5, NA)
> prod(x)
```

```
[1] NA
```

```
> prod(x, na.rm = TRUE)
```

```
[1] 15
```

The second version removes the missing value from x before taking the product. One of the main reasons for getting NA as the result of an operation where you did not expect it is that the na.rm argument has not been set to TRUE.[13] You are also informed about this feature in the *Details* section, which generally provides more in-depth information about an object and its particularities. The section *Value* exactly describes what is returned from the function, namely a vector of length one—the product. The *Examples* section provides minimal, and sometimes not so minimal, working examples. Just copy the example from the help page into the editor.

---

[13] This often happens with the mean() function, for example.

```
> print(prod(1:7)) == print(gamma(8))
```

```
[1] 5040
[1] 5040
[1] TRUE
```

The print() function is a generic function for printing its arguments into the console. As it is used twice, the first two objects that appear as printed output in the console are the results of each print() function's argument. Both expressions yield the same number, so the logical operator == returns the value TRUE as the third output that results from the entire expression.

The help.start() function automatically opens the HTML version of the general R help page, from which you can proceed further.[14] The advantage of the HTML version over the text version is the availability of links for jumping directly to related topics.

---

[14] You can also use the menu in the RGui window: *Help→HTML Help*.

Chapter 3
Crisp-Set QCA

Abstract A QCA which uses only binary-value crisp-set data is referred to as a crisp-set QCA (csQCA). In this chapter, the findings of Krook's (2010) csQCA study on women's representation in national parliaments are replicated. We first show how to calibrate crisp sets from categorical and continuous base variables, using both external criteria as suggested by theoretical knowledge and internal criteria as arrived at through empirical data analysis. We then proceed to the testing of necessity relations. The analysis of sufficiency relations is the next step, including the derivation of complex, parsimonious and intermediate solutions. Finally, we also demonstrate how to plot results for both types of relation as Venn diagrams.

3.1 Calibrating Crisp Sets

The process of getting from base variable values (also called *raw data*) to condition or outcome set membership scores is referred to as *calibration*. In this section, we demonstrate how to calibrate crisp sets from raw data of categorical and continuous base variables. Both *external* and *internal calibration criteria* will be used in this process. External criteria result from prior theoretical knowledge, whereas internal criteria follow from the empirical analysis of the data at hand. The raw data presented in Table 1, Krook (2010, p. 893), should first be downloaded from the bibliography section at http://www.compasss.org. It should then be loaded into R as shown above in Sect. 2.2, and be assigned to the data frame object KrookRaw.

```
> KrookRaw <- read.table("Krook2010raw.txt", header = TRUE,
+   row.names = "Country")
> KrookRaw

     es  qu     ws     wm  lp   wnp
SE   PR  Yes  SocDem   Non   5  47.3
FI   PR  No   SocDem   Non   5  42.0
```

A. Thiem and A. Duşa, *Qualitative Comparative Analysis with R*,
SpringerBriefs in Political Science, DOI: 10.1007/978-1-4614-4584-5_3,
© The Author(s) 2013

```
NO      PR Yes  SocDem Autonom 14 37.9
..      .. ...  ...... ....... .. ....
```
<<rest omitted>>

There is data for 22 countries on five variables, these being the type of the electoral system (*es*: PR, mixed, and majority), whether or not the country has quotas for women (*qu*: Yes, No), qualitative distinctions between welfare states in offering women social and economic opportunities (*ws*: social-democratic, conservative, liberal), women's movements' degree of autonomy from the state and political parties (*wm*: non, autonomous), the percentage of parliamentary seats held by left-libertarian parties in 2002 (*lp*), and the dependent variable measuring the proportion of women in the single or lower house of parliament (*wnp*).[1] In order to get from the raw data presented in Table 1, Krook (2010, p. 893) to the crisp-set data shown in Table 2, Krook (2010, p. 895), informed choices regarding the calibration of the target sets must be made.[2] As a preparatory step, we first create a new empty data frame—call it Krook—with the data.frame() function.

```
> Krook <- data.frame(matrix(rep(numeric(22), 6), nrow = 22,
+   dimnames = list(row.names(KrookRaw),
+   toupper(names(KrookRaw))))))
```

Inside data.frame(), the matrix() function is used to setup a matrix with 22 (rows) times 6 (columns) numeric elements using the rep() function. A list of two elements is passed to the dimnames argument, the first for the row names and the second for the column names. The row names of Krook are the same as the row names of KrookRaw, and the column names for Krook are extracted from KrookRaw using the names() function. The enclosing function toupper() then converts the lower case variable names from KrookRaw to upper case set names.[3]

Krook now applies the following rules to the four categorical variables *es*, *qu*, *ws*, and *wm* in order to calibrate the associated target condition sets **ES**, **QU**, **WS**, and **WM**: countries with PR electoral systems are coded "1", all others "0"; countries with a quota are coded "1" and "0" otherwise; social democratic welfare states are coded "1", all others "0"; and countries with autonomous women's movements are coded "1" and "0" otherwise. An efficient solution for this kind of recoding is provided by the ifelse() function, which takes three arguments: a test, a value if the test returns true, and a value if the test returns false.

```
> Krook$ES <- ifelse(KrookRaw$es == "PR", 1, 0)
> Krook$QU <- ifelse(KrookRaw$qu == "Yes", 1, 0)
> Krook$WS <- ifelse(KrookRaw$ws == "SocDem", 1, 0)
> Krook$WM <- ifelse(KrookRaw$wm == "Autonom", 1, 0)
```

The dataset Krook should start to look more like Table 2 now.

---

[1] Some variable and set labels have been adapted for this replication.

[2] Note that Krook calls Table 3.2 a truth table, which it is not yet.

[3] If Krook is now called up, it can be seen that all entries are zeros. This is just a standard value for filling generic objects of data type numeric.

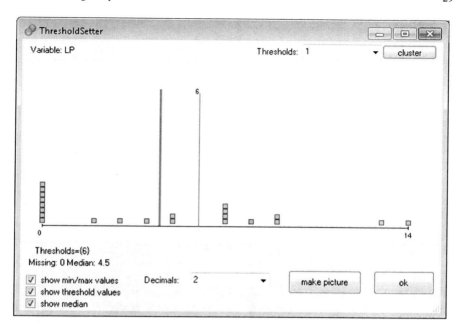

Fig. 3.1 Threshold-setter window in Tosmana

```
> Krook

    ES QU WS WM LP WNP
SE   1  1  1  0  0   0
FI   1  0  1  0  0   0
NO   1  1  1  1  0   0
..   .  .  .  .  .   .
<<rest omitted>>
```

This leaves the condition **LP** and the outcome **WNP** to be calibrated from the ratio-scaled variables *lp* and *wnp*. Krook mentions that Tosmana possesses a very user-friendly feature: the threshold-setter. It is shown for *lp* in Fig. 3.1.

Thresholds are the breakpoints that separate particular groups of data from each other in the calibration process. The threshold-setter window visualizes the distribution of cases in a bar chart and if the user wishes so, the threshold-setter function suggests up to nine thresholds for calibrating condition values based on a cluster analysis of the data. Visualizing distributions of cases is just as easy in R and almost always already provides all the information users require in order to make informed decisions about how to find suitable thresholds for calibrating sets when a justified theoretical argument is unavailable.

Bar charts are ideal for a limited number of (usually categorical) values. They can be created in R with the `barplot()` function. If the data to be plotted comes from a vector of values, then the heights of the bars reflect these values. If the data comes

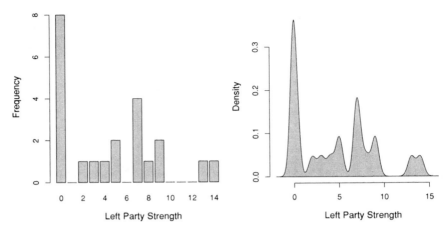

Fig. 3.2 Bar chart (*left*) and density plot (*right*) of Left party strength

from a matrix of values, then each bar will be a stack of individual bars reflecting each value in each column of the data.[4] An object containing all potential data values with a count of each value occurrence is a one-dimensional table. In order for the plot not to be limited only to those values which exist in the data, but the entire range, a categorical variable containing all values is required. These variables are referred to in R as factors and include nominally (unordered) as well as ordinally-scaled variables (ordered). Tables can be created with the `table()` function, factors with the `factor()` function, whose argument `levels` specifies the different categories.

```
> (tab <- table(factor(KrookRaw$lp, levels = 0:14)))

 0  1  2  3  4  5  6  7  8  9 10 11 12 13 14
 8  0  1  1  1  2  0  4  1  2  0  0  0  1  1
```

The factor has 15 levels because left party strength ranges from 0 to 14 %. Levels 1, 6, and 10–12 do not occur. All that remains to be done is to pass the table to the `barplot()` function. The result is shown in the left panel of Fig. 3.2.

```
> barplot(tab, xlab = "Left Party Strength",
+   ylab = "Frequency")
```

The two arguments `xlab` and `ylab` specify the axes labels. They are available for most types of plots in R. In contrast, if the data is truly continuous and/or can be conceived of as representing draws from a variable with a probability density, a kernel density plot is a very suitable means of visualization and often more effective than a histogram.

---

[4] For example, Fig. 1.1 has been created by `barplot()` with a matrix of data in which each column represents the year of publication and each row one of the three QCA variants.

```
> LPdens <- density(KrookRaw$lp, bw = 0.4)
> plot(LPdens, xlab = "Left Party Strength", ylab = "Density")
> polygon(LPdens, col = "gray")
```

The density() function is first applied to create the object LPdens, using its argument bw for a smoothing bandwidth of 0.4. This object is then passed to the plot() function. Finally, the polygon() function fills the area under the density curve.[5] The result is shown in the right panel of Fig. 3.2.

If an appropriate threshold has still not been found even after having exhausted all the means presented above, other formal methods may be employed. In order to aid in the search for a threshold, Tosmana also shows the median and the suggested cluster-analytical threshold value in addition to the bar chart. The median and arithmetic mean of an empirical distribution of data can be found with the eponymous functions.

```
> median(KrookRaw$lp)
```

```
[1] 4.5
```

```
> mean(KrookRaw$lp)
```

```
[1] 4.545455
```

A last resort solution is to perform hierarchical cluster analysis with QCA's findTh() function. By default, it returns a suitable threshold for dividing the data into two groups. Further arguments besides the number of groups are the clustering method hclustm and the distance measure distm.[6]

Full syntax:

```
> findTh(KrookRaw$lp, groups = 2, hclustm = "complete",
+  distm = "euclidean")
```

```
> findTh(KrookRaw$lp)
```

```
[1] 6
```

```
> findTh(KrookRaw$wnp)
```

```
[1] 28.3
```

Although findTh() suggests that 6% be chosen as the threshold in *lp* and 28% in *wnp*, Krook (2010) opts for 7 and 30%. The calibration of crisp sets is achieved

---

[5] The graphics device showing the density plot must not be closed before the polygon() function has been evaluated.

[6] See ?hclust and ?dist for all argument values of hclustm and distm.

in QCA with the `calibrate()` function. For csQCA, it takes two mandatory arguments: the base variable to be transformed and a numeric vector of thresholds provided in the `thresholds` argument, which simplifies to a scalar in our case. The logical argument `include` indicates whether the threshold should be included into or excluded from the target set. All remaining arguments are only relevant for fsQCA and will be explained later in Chap. 4.

Full syntax:

```
> calibrate(KrookRaw$lp, type = "crisp", thresholds = 7,
+   include = TRUE, logistic = FALSE, idm = 0.95,
+   ecdf = FALSE, p = 1, q = 1)
```

```
> Krook$LP <- calibrate(KrookRaw$lp, thresholds = 7)
> Krook$WNP <- calibrate(KrookRaw$wnp, thresholds = 30)
```

The dataset now looks exactly like Table 2, Krook (2010, p. 895).

```
> Krook
```

	ES	QU	WS	WM	LP	WNP
SE	1	1	1	0	0	1
FI	1	0	1	0	0	1
NO	1	1	1	1	1	1
..	.	.	.	.	.	.

```
<<rest omitted>>
```

All sets have now been calibrated.[7] The next step is to test for the existence of necessity relations between condition and outcome sets.

3.2 Testing for Necessity

Analyses of necessity should precede those of sufficiency (Ragin 2000, p. 106). In the first section, we present common parameters of fit on which the analysis of necessity relations in the second section is based. In the third section, we show how to produce Venn diagrams for visualizing these relations.

---

[7] The completely calibrated dataset is also integrated in the QCA package. Type `data(Krook)` to load it. This will overwrite the current object with the same name.

Table 3.1 Necessity in csQCA

		1	①	②
O			relevant cases inclusion ↓	relevant cases
		0	③ irrelevant cases	④ relevant cases coverage ↓
			0	1
			C	

3.2.1 Parameters of Fit

Analyses of necessity proceed from the observation of the outcome **O** to the observation of the condition(s) **C**. For analyzing necessity inclusion, the decisive question is how often **C** has been present, given the presence of **O**, in relation to the overall presence of **O**. For analyzing necessity coverage, in contrast, the crucial question is how often **C** has been present, given the presence of **O**, in relation to the overall presence of **C**. If necessity inclusion is high enough, the evidence is consistent with the hypothesis that **C** is necessary for **O** (**C** ← **O**). If necessity coverage within such a relation is high enough, the evidence is consistent with the hypothesis that **C** is not trivially necessary for **O**. Table 3.1 shows the relevant cells for necessity inclusion and necessity coverage of **C**.

Cell ② is relevant for both inclusion and coverage, while cell ① is only relevant for inclusion and cell ④ only for coverage. The more cases fall into cells ① and ④, *ceteris paribus*, the more inclusion and coverage will decrease. Cell ③ is irrelevant for either measure. The necessity inclusion of **C**, $\mathrm{Incl}_N(\mathbf{C})$, is calculated as given in Eq. (3.1).

$$\mathrm{Incl}_N(\mathbf{C}) = \frac{\sum_{i=1}^{n} c_i = 1 | o_i = 1}{\sum_{i=1}^{n} o_i = 1} \tag{3.1}$$

The necessity coverage of **C**, $\mathrm{Cov}_N(\mathbf{C})$, is calculated as given in Eq. (3.2).

$$\mathrm{Cov}_N(\mathbf{C}) = \frac{\sum_{i=1}^{n} c_i = 1 | o_i = 1}{\sum_{i=1}^{n} c_i = 1} \tag{3.2}$$

3.2.2 Analyzing Necessity Relations

In order to test for necessary conditions, QCA provides the superSubset() function. This returns inclusion, PRI, and coverage scores for those of the $3^k - 1$ combinations of k conditions which optimally fit the given cut-offs for inclusion and coverage.[8]

---

[8] In csQCA and mvQCA, PRI equals inclusion. We thus ignore PRI in the remainder of this chapter and come back to it in more detail in Sect. 4.2.1.

Therefore, superSubset() does not require a preselection of the combinations to be tested, and so removes the risk of leaving potentially interesting results undiscovered.[9] The theoretical idea behind superSubset() is simple. Starting with the $2k$ uniliteral combinations $C_1, c_1, C_2, c_2, \ldots, C_k, c_k$, the number of literals in those combinations that meet the cut-offs is incrementally increased from 1 to k until their scores fall below the cut-offs.

If, for example, the uniliteral combination C_1 passes the inclusion cut-off, it can be combined with all of the other $2k - 2$ uniliteral combinations to form the next more complex conjunctive combinations $C_1 \cdot C_2$ to $C_1 \cdot c_k$.[10] If the biliteral combination $C_1 \cdot C_2$ still passes the inclusion cut-off, it can be further combined with all of the remaining $2k - 4$ uniliteral combinations to form the next more complex triliteral combinations $C_1 \cdot C_2 \cdot C_3$ to $C_1 \cdot C_2 \cdot c_k$, and so on. This process can continue until the inclusion score of some combination falls below the given cut-off for some number of literals g. Only then will the coverage cut-off be evaluated. In other words, the inclusion cut-off always enjoys priority over the coverage cut-off. Combinations with more than g literals will always fall below the inclusion cut-off, whereby the need to further evaluate coverage is also removed. All g-literal combinations as well as all less complex combinations will therefore be returned by superSubset().[11]

Situation may occur when no uniliteral combination passes the inclusion cut-off. When this happens, disjunctive instead of conjunctive combinations are searched. If, for example, C_1 does not pass the inclusion cut-off, it can be combined with all of the other $2k - 2$ uniliteral combinations to form the next more complex biliteral combination $C_1 + C_2$ to $C_1 + c_k$. If the biliteral combination $C_1 + C_2$ still does not exceed the cut-off, it can be further augmented until the cut-off is passed for some number of literals g, or the maximally-complex k-literal combination has been formed. In contrast to the presence of at least biliteral conjunctive combinations, only the g-literal disjunctive combinations thus found are returned by superSubset(), but neither less nor more complex combinations because combinations with more than g literals will always exceed the inclusion cut-off.

Full syntax:

```
> superSubset(Krook, outcome = "WNP", neg.out = FALSE,
+   conditions = c("ES", "QU", "WS", "WM", "LP"),
+   relation = "necessity", incl.cut = 0.9, cov.cut = 0.52,
+   use.tilde = FALSE, use.letters = FALSE)
```

---

[9] Such a result is presented in Sect. 4.2.2.

[10] There are $2k - 2$ uniliteral combinations left because no condition can be combined with its own negation.

[11] Computationally, superSubset() does not use the procedure described above, but immediately creates all $3^k - 1$ combinations from which it then extracts only those which fit the criteria.

```
> KrookNR <- superSubset(Krook, outcome = "WNP",
+   incl.cut = 0.9, cov.cut = 0.52)
> KrookNR
```

		incl	PRI	cov.r
1	wm+LP	0.909	0.909	0.667
2	WS+LP	0.909	0.909	0.909
3	WS+WM	0.909	0.909	0.625
4	QU+LP	0.909	0.909	0.526
5	QU+WS	0.909	0.909	0.556
6	ES+LP	1.000	1.000	0.733
7	ES+WM	1.000	1.000	0.524
8	ES+qu	0.909	0.909	0.625
9	ES+QU	0.909	0.909	0.526
10	qu+WM+LP	0.909	0.909	0.588
11	QU+WM+lp	1.000	1.000	0.524

The first argument is the data frame (or matrix) of set data. If the conditions are not specified, superSubset() will choose in their place all sets in the data but the outcome. By default, the type of relation to be tested is that of necessity as specified by the argument relation, the inclusion cut-off argument incl.cut is set to 1, and that for coverage cov.cut to 0. When neg.out = TRUE, the outcome is negated. By default, results are presented in upper and lower case notation, but for non-multi-value data, negation by tilde can be achieved with the logical argument use.tilde. The argument use.letters converts set names to letters in alphabetical order. For a better overview, the returned combinations are listed in increasing order of complexity.

3.2.3 Plotting Results

Venn diagrams are a suitable means to visualize results from a csQCA (Dușa 2007b). Tosmana offers extensive features in this respect, but Venn diagrams can also be generated in R, for example with the VennDiagram package (Chen 2012).[12] It should first be installed and loaded as shown in Sect. 2.2. Below we demonstrate how to plot the three biliteral combinations **WS + LP**, **ES + LP**, and **ES + WM**, which were found by superSubset() to have particularly high inclusion and coverage scores given their low complexity. For this purpose, we use VennDiagram's venn.diagram()

---

[12] Internal functionality for Venn diagrams is foreseen in a future update of QCA.

function.[13] Before proceeding, we introduce another feature of `superSubset()` which simplifies the generation of Venn diagrams.

Besides presenting the user with combinations of conditions and their parameters of fit, the `superSubset()` function also generates an invisible component called `coms`. This component contains each case's <u>com</u>bination <u>m</u>embership <u>s</u>cores. As `coms` is a data frame, all columns can be accessed as shown in Sect. 2.8.

```
> (COms <- KrookNR$coms[ , 1:9])
```

	wm+LP	WS+LP	WS+WM	QU+LP	QU+WS	ES+LP	ES+WM	ES+qu	ES+QU
SE	1	1	1	1	1	1	1	1	1
FI	1	1	1	0	1	1	1	1	1
NO	1	1	1	1	1	1	1	1	1
..	.	.	.	.	.	.	.	.	.

```
<<rest omitted>>
```

With the `coms` component of `superSubset()`, users are spared from long Boolean calculations applying the `pmin()` and `pmax()` functions. The three combinations can now easily be plotted by combining the `COms` object with the `venn.diagram()` function.

```
> library("VennDiagram")
> vennKrookNec <- venn.diagram(
+   x = list(
+     "WNP" = which(Krook$WNP == 1),
+     "WS+LP" = which(COms[ , 2] == 1),
+     "ES+LP" = which(COms[ , 6] == 1),
+     "ES+WM" = which(COms[ , 7] == 1)),
+   filename = NULL,
+   cex = 2.5, cat.cex = 2, cat.pos = c(350, 10, 0, 0),
+   cat.dist = c(0.22, 0.22, 0.12, 0.12),
+   fill = gray(c(0.3, 0.5, 0.7, 0.9))
+ )
> grid.draw(vennKrookNec)
```

The `venn.diagram()` function takes a list of vectors, each of which represents a different set. However, Venn diagrams require the data to be in the format of an *incidence table*, such that each element in the diagram contains the number of cases for each pairing of combinations. The columns in `Krook` can therefore not be directly passed to the function. In order to produce such an incidence table on the fly, a very handy R function called `which()` is available. It extracts the row numbers of all elements from a data frame for which some conditional statement is true. For creating the ellipse that represents the outcome **WNP**, the row numbers of all cases

---

[13] The VennDiagram package only supports diagrams of order four. With more sets, its authors argue, Venn diagrams become too complex for intuitive visualization (Chen and Boutros 2011, p. 37).

Fig. 3.3 Venn diagram of
three necessity relations in
csQCA

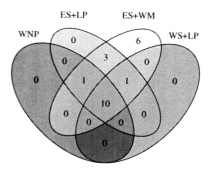

for which **WNP** is present need to be extracted. The original set data frame Krook
should be used for this purpose. The ellipses for the three disjunctive combinations
to be intersected with **WNP** are formed likewise, but with the column-indexed object
COms.[14]

The filename argument is mandatory. If a simple filename is provided, the figure
will be saved in the working directory.[15] Currently, only *.tiff* images can be produced in this way, but *.tiff* is a common format for publication-quality figures. If the
filename argument is set to NULL, the object can be directly displayed in the usual
R plotting device with the grid.draw() function and be saved anywhere in one of
the available formats (*.pdf*, *.png*, *.jpg*, etc.).

All arguments after the filename determine the exact appearance of the diagram,
including the size of the area labels (cex), the size of the set labels (cat.cex), the
position of each set name in degrees (cat.pos), the distance of the set labels from
the edge of the set circle (cat.dist), and the color of each circle (fill).[16] The
resulting Venn diagram is shown in Fig. 3.3.

Eleven cases are in **WNP**, all of which are also in **ES + WM** and **ES + LP**, but
only ten of which are also in **WS + LP**. If the identification of this remaining case
was of interest, the rownames() function could be used in conjunction with a logical
index.

```
> rownames(Krook)[which(Krook$WS != 1 & Krook$LP != 1 &
+   Krook$WNP == 1)]
```

```
[1] "ES"
```

Spain is the only case that falls out of the subset relation.

---

[14] Alternatively, the full name of the combination could have been used instead. For example,
COms[, 2] is equivalent to COms$"WS+LP".

[15] See Sect. 2.11 for how to find and set the working directory.

[16] Enter ?VennDiagram for more details.

Table 3.2 Sufficiency in csQCA	1	O	① relevant cases coverage ↓	② relevant cases
	0		③ irrelevant cases	④ relevant cases inclusion ↓
			0	1
			C	

3.3 Testing for Sufficiency

The ultimate goal of QCA is to analyze set-theoretic sufficiency relations (Ragin 2009, p. 110) for which the construction of the truth table is central. In addition to the exhaustive formation of all configurations, an outcome value for each configuration has to be established. The outcome value is a fractional truth value of the statement that the configuration is sufficient for the outcome to occur.

3.3.1 Parameters of Fit

Analyses of sufficiency proceed from the observation of some condition(s) $\mathbf{C}$ to the observation of the outcome $\mathbf{O}$. For analyzing sufficiency inclusion, the decisive question is how often $\mathbf{O}$ has been present, given the presence of $\mathbf{C}$, in relation to the overall presence of $\mathbf{C}$. For analyzing sufficiency coverage, in contrast, the crucial question is how often $\mathbf{O}$ has been present, given the presence of $\mathbf{C}$, in relation to the overall presence of $\mathbf{O}$. If sufficiency inclusion is high enough, the evidence is consistent with the hypothesis that $\mathbf{C}$ is sufficient for $\mathbf{O}$ ($\mathbf{C} \rightarrow \mathbf{O}$). If sufficiency coverage within such a relation is high enough, the evidence is consistent with the hypothesis that $\mathbf{C}$ is not trivially sufficient for $\mathbf{O}$. Table 3.2 shows the relevant cells for sufficiency inclusion and sufficiency coverage of $\mathbf{C}$.

Cell ② is relevant for both inclusion and coverage, while cell ① is only relevant for coverage and cell ④ only for inclusion. The more cases fall into cells ① and ④, *ceteris paribus*, the more coverage and inclusion will decrease. Cell ③ is irrelevant for either measure. The sufficiency inclusion of $\mathbf{C}$, $\mathrm{Incl}_S(\mathbf{C})$, is calculated as given in Eq. (3.3).

$$\mathrm{Incl}_S(\mathbf{C}) = \frac{\sum_{i=1}^{n} o_i = 1 | c_i = 1}{\sum_{i=1}^{n} c_i = 1} \qquad (3.3)$$

The sufficiency coverage of $\mathbf{C}$, $\mathrm{Cov}_S(\mathbf{C})$, is calculated as given in Eq. (3.4).

$$\mathrm{Cov}_S(\mathbf{C}) = \frac{\sum_{i=1}^{n} o_i = 1 | c_i = 1}{\sum_{i=1}^{n} o_i = 1} \qquad (3.4)$$

3.3.2 Constructing the Truth Table

The `truthTable()` function constructs truth tables from crisp-set data. At the very least, it requires two arguments: a matrix or data frame of crisp-set membership scores and an outcome set. In order to create the truth table object `KrookTT`, the dataset `Krook` is specified as the first argument, then the outcome set **WNP**. If not all columns except the one representing the outcome set are to be selected as conditions, the `conditions` argument must also be specified. As all sets but **WNP** are conditions, this argument need not be provided.

Full syntax:

```
> KrookTT <- truthTable(Krook, outcome = "WNP", neg.out = FALSE,
+   conditions = c("ES", "QU", "WS", "WM", "LP"), n.cut = 1,
+   incl.cut1 = 1, incl.cut0 = 1, complete = FALSE,
+   show.cases = TRUE, sort.by = c("incl", "n"),
+   decreasing = TRUE, use.letters = FALSE)
```

```
> KrookTT <- truthTable(Krook, outcome = "WNP",
+   show.cases = TRUE, sort.by = c("incl", "n"))
> KrookTT
```

```
 OUT: outcome value
   n: number of cases in configuration
incl: sufficiency inclusion score
 PRI: proportional reduction in inconsistency
```

	ES	QU	WS	WM	LP	OUT	n	incl	PRI	cases
28	1	1	0	1	1	1	2	1.000	1.000	NL,BE
32	1	1	1	1	1	1	2	1.000	1.000	NO,IS
4	0	0	0	1	1	1	1	1.000	1.000	NZ
12	0	1	0	1	1	1	1	1.000	1.000	DE
21	1	0	1	0	0	1	1	1.000	1.000	FI
24	1	0	1	1	1	1	1	1.000	1.000	DK
26	1	1	0	0	1	1	1	1.000	1.000	AT
27	1	1	0	1	0	1	1	1.000	1.000	ES
29	1	1	1	0	0	1	1	1.000	1.000	SE
11	0	1	0	1	0	0	4	0.000	0.000	AU,GB,FR,IE
25	1	1	0	0	0	0	3	0.000	0.000	CH,PT,GR
3	0	0	0	1	0	0	2	0.000	0.000	CA,US
9	0	1	0	0	0	0	1	0.000	0.000	IT
18	1	0	0	0	1	0	1	0.000	0.000	LU

The truthTable() function includes three cut-off arguments that influence how a configuration is coded in the outcome value column "OUT": n.cut, incl.cut1 and incl.cut0. The first argument n.cut specifies the minimum number of cases needed in order to not code a configuration as a logical remainder as indicated by "?". The second argument incl.cut1 specifies the minimal sufficiency inclusion score for a non-remainder configuration to be coded as true ("1"). The third argument incl.cut0 offers the possibility of coding configurations as contradictions ("C") when their inclusion score is neither high nor low enough to consider them as true, respectively false. If the inclusion score of a non-remainder configuration falls below incl.cut0, it is always coded false ("0").

By default, truthTable() only returns those configurations of the truth table in which at least n.cut cases have membership. The names of these cases are printed if the show.cases argument is set to TRUE. With the sort.by argument, the truth table can also be ordered along inclusion scores, numbers of cases, or both. The logical argument decreasing controls the sorting order.

3.3.3 Boolean Minimization

The minimization of the canonical sum whose fundamental products correspond to all true configurations yields the *complex solution*. The derivation of this solution type is achieved with the eqmcc() function (enhanced Quine-McCluskey) (Duşa 2007a, 2010). It is the core function of the **QCA** package.

```
Full syntax:

> KrookSC <- eqmcc(KrookTT, explain = "1", include = "1",
+    all.sol = FALSE, omit = c(), direxp = c(), rowdom = TRUE,
+    details = TRUE, show.cases = FALSE, use.tilde = FALSE,
+    use.letters = FALSE)
```

```
> KrookSC <- eqmcc(KrookTT, details = TRUE,
+    show.cases = TRUE)
```

The truth table object KrookTT is passed to eqmcc() as the first argument.[17] By default, true configurations are explained. No additional information is required for arriving at the complex solution. The all.sol argument causes eqmcc() to derive all minimal sums of the solution, not just those with the fewest PIs.[18] The logical argument details causes all parameters of fit to be printed together with

---

[17] The eqmcc() function can also directly process datasets with crisp-set membership scores. However, it is recommended that the function only be used after having created and evaluated the truth table.

[18] This argument has been suggested by Michael Baumgartner.

the minimal sum: inclusion, PRI, raw coverage, and unique coverage scores for each prime implicant (PI) as well as the minimal sum.[19] If details = TRUE, the logical argument show.cases also prints the names of the cases that are covered by each PI.

```
> KrookSC

n OUT = 1/0/C: 11/11/0
  Total        : 22


Number of multiple-covered cases: 2

S1: ES*QU*ws*LP + ES*QU*ws*WM + es*ws*WM*LP + ES*WS*wm*lp +
    ES*WS*WM*LP


                 incl   PRI    cov.r  cov.u  cases
    -----------------------------------------------------
1   ES*QU*ws*LP  1.000  1.000  0.273  0.091  NL,BE; AT
2   ES*QU*ws*WM  1.000  1.000  0.273  0.091  NL,BE; ES
3   es*ws*WM*LP  1.000  1.000  0.182  0.182  NZ; DE
4   ES*WS*wm*lp  1.000  1.000  0.182  0.182  FI; SE
5   ES*WS*WM*LP  1.000  1.000  0.273  0.273  NO,IS; DK
    -----------------------------------------------------

    S1           1.000  1.000  1.000
```

The output which is printed when an object returned by eqmcc() is called up consists of three parts. The header provides information about the number of cases in each of the three types of configurations and the total number of cases. If show.cases = TRUE, it also displays the number of cases which are covered by more than one PI. The middle part prints the solution, which may consist of one or more minimal sums S. The bottom part provides the parameters-of-fit (POF) table.

The minimal sum consists of five PIs. These cover 11 cases, namely the Netherlands, Belgium, Austria, Spain, New Zealand, Germany, Finland, Sweden, Norway, Iceland, and Denmark. The Netherlands and Belgium are covered by multiple PIs as indicated above the POF table. Cases from the same configuration are separated by a comma, those from different configurations by a semicolon.

3.3.4 Incorporating Logical Remainders

Logical remainders are configurations which are not populated by any cases, or too few cases. However, instead of forming the useless tail of the truth table, each single such configuration provides a potentially relevant combination of conditions that allows researchers to engage in counterfactual thinking. Two common solution types

---

[19] Unique coverage scores do not apply to minimal sums.

which rely on counterfactuals are the parsimonious and the intermediate solution. Before logical remainders can be incorporated into the analysis, a new object which contains the entire truth table should be created. The provision of the additional argument complete = TRUE in truthTable() generates the entire truth table. For reasons of space, it is not called up here.

```
> KrookTT <- truthTable(Krook, outcome = "WNP",
+   complete = TRUE, sort.by = c("incl", "n"))
```

With KrookTT now containing the complete truth table, it becomes possible to generate solution types which incorporate logical remainders.

3.3.4.1 Parsimonious Solution

If all logical remainders are made available for minimization, the minimal sum(s) obtained from this process are summarized under the *parsimonious solution*. Logical remainders can be incorporated into the minimization process by using the include argument in eqmcc(). Ignore the rowdom argument for the moment.

```
> KrookSP <- eqmcc(KrookTT, include = "?", rowdom = FALSE,
+   details = TRUE)
> KrookSP

n OUT = 1/0/C: 11/11/0
   Total     : 22

S1: WS + ES*WM + QU*LP + (es*LP)
S2: WS + ES*WM + QU*LP + (WM*LP)
```

		incl	PRI	cov.r	cov.u	(S1)	(S2)
1	WS	1.000	1.000	0.455	0.182	0.182	0.182
2	ES*WM	1.000	1.000	0.545	0.091	0.091	0.091
3	QU*LP	1.000	1.000	0.545	0.091	0.091	0.091
4	es*LP	1.000	1.000	0.182	0.000	0.091	
5	WM*LP	1.000	1.000	0.636	0.000		0.091
	S1	1.000	1.000	1.000			
	S2	1.000	1.000	1.000			

The parsimonious solution consists of the two minimal sums S_1 and S_2, each of which contains four PIs. This situation is the analogy of choosing all inessential PIs in the PI chart of fs/QCA with the *Mark All* button in the bottom-left part of the window. It is shown in Fig. 3.4. The *Data* line in this window indicates that the

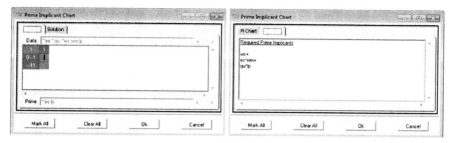

Fig. 3.4 PI chart window (Krook) in fs/QCA

fundamental product $es \cdot qu \cdot ws \cdot WM \cdot LP$ is covered by *Prime* $es \cdot LP$ as well as $WM \cdot LP$. These two PIs are not listed in the *Solution* tab, which shows all essential PIs, but at least one is required to complete a minimal sum, so users are asked to choose one of the inessential PIs or both.

In QCA's solution output, inessential PIs are enclosed by brackets and listed in the middle part on the POF table, while essential PIs are listed in the upper part. The bottom part shows all parameters of fit for each minimal sum. If there are multiple minimal sums, unique coverage may vary, for both essential and inessential PIs. The columns with the respective header for each minimal sum are therefore listed next to the unique coverage column cov.u.

Although there is nothing wrong in choosing both inessential PIs, $WM \cdot LP$ in fact dominates $es \cdot LP$. One PI P_1 is said to dominate another P_2 if all fundamental products covered by P_2 are also covered by P_1 and both are not interchangeable. This principle is often referred to as *row dominance* because in PI charts, columns represent fundamental products, and rows the PIs. The application of the row dominance principle is controlled through the rowdom argument in eqmcc(). When set to its default value TRUE, dominated PI are always eliminated from the solution. When set to FALSE, dominated PIs are retained.[20]

That $WM \cdot LP$ really dominates $es \cdot LP$ in the parsimonious solution can be seen when calling up the subcomponent p.sol in the PI chart component PIchart of the QCA solution object created by eqmcc().

```
> KrookSP$PIchart$p.sol
```

	28	32	4	12	21	24	26	27	29
WS	-	x	-	-	x	x	-	-	x
es*LP	-	-	x	x	-	-	-	-	-
ES*WM	x	x	-	-	-	x	-	x	-
QU*LP	x	x	-	x	-	-	x	-	-
WM*LP	x	x	x	x	-	x	-	-	-
ES*qu*lp	-	-	-	-	x	-	-	-	-
qu*wm*lp	-	-	-	-	x	-	-	-	-

---

[20] It may happen that there are multiple inessential PIs, none of which dominates the other.

Truth table rows 4 and 12 are implied by **es** · **LP**, but so they are by **WM** · **LP**. Both PIs are not interchangeable because **WM** · **LP** also implies truth table rows 24, 28, and 32 in addition. As row 12 is also implied by **QU** · **LP**, row 4 must correspond to the fundamental product for which **es** · **LP** and **WM** · **LP** are alternatives. Using this row name, the configuration in question can be found by accessing the `tt` component of the truth table object. We also index the columns because only the raw configuration is of interest.[21]

```
> KrookTT$tt["4", 1:5]

  ES QU WS WM LP
4  0  0  0  1  1
```

Although Krook provides both minimal sums in her study, S_2 shall be chosen for further analysis here because **WM** · **LP** not only dominates **es** · **LP** but it is also more in line with theoretical expectations. In this regard, the simplifying assumptions (SA) on which the derivation of the parsimonious solution has been based may also be of interest. The SAs of S_2 can be called up by accessing its subcomponent in the overall list component SA returned by `eqmcc()`.

```
> KrookSP$SA$S2

  ES QU WS WM LP
5  0  0  1  0  0
6  0  0  1  0  1
7  0  0  1  1  0
.  .  .  .  .  .
<<rest omitted>>
```

Fifteen logical remainders have been used as SAs in the derivation of S_2.

3.3.4.2 Intermediate Solution

If researchers make explicit assumptions about the set-theoretic relationship between a condition and the outcome by formulating *directional expectations*, the result is called the *intermediate solution*. The intermediate solution is always a subset of the parsimonious solution, so it does not use any logical remainders as simplifying assumptions other than those which have already been used in the derivation of the parsimonious solution. The complex and the parsimonious solution are always unique, but the intermediate solution is not. Essentially, it consists of the entire set of possible solutions between the complex and the parsimonious solution. In fs/QCA, the window where directional expectations are specified is shown in Fig. 3.5. Radio buttons specify whether there is an expectation, and if so, which direction it has.

---

[21] It is important to use double quotes around the number 4 because row names are of data type *character*. Alternatively, truth table rows can also be accessed in the solution object. The same output would have been generated by `KrookSP$tt$tt["4", 1:5]`.

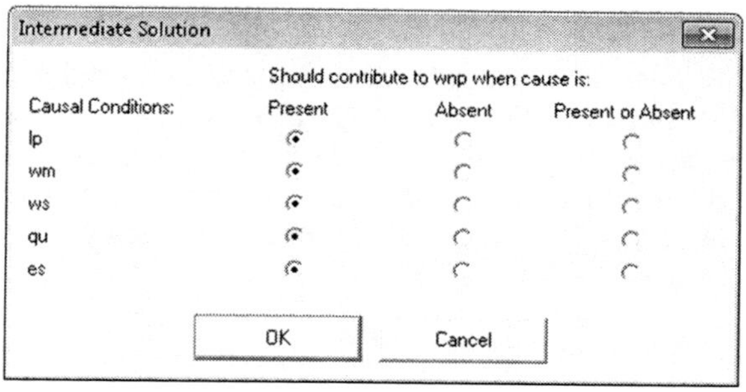

Fig. 3.5 Directional expectations window in fs/QCA

Intermediate solutions can be generated in QCA by making use of the `direxp` argument. This takes a numeric vector whose length and order equals the number and arrangement of conditions in the truth table. The value "1" indicates that the condition is expected to contribute to an outcome value of "1", "0" that it is the negation of this condition. The value "−1" indicates that no directional expectations are made. Krook does not provide an intermediate solution, so we extend her analysis here. The relationship between each single condition and the outcome value is assumed to be positive, which means that **ES, QU, WS, WM,** and **LP** are expected to contribute to OUT = 1 in their presence. Instead of writing out `direxp = c(1,1,1,1,1)`, the `rep()` function, introduced in Sect. 2.5, offers a slightly more efficient solution.

```
> KrookSI <- eqmcc(KrookTT, include = "?", direxp = rep(1, 5),
+   details = TRUE)
> KrookSI

n OUT = 1/0/C: 11/11/0
  Total      : 22

p.sol: WS + ES*WM + QU*LP + WM*LP

S1:    ES*WS + WM*LP + ES*QU*LP + ES*QU*WM

                incl    PRI     cov.r   cov.u
---------------------------------------------
1  ES*WS        1.000   1.000   0.455   0.182
2  WM*LP        1.000   1.000   0.636   0.182
3  ES*QU*LP     1.000   1.000   0.455   0.091
4  ES*QU*WM     1.000   1.000   0.455   0.091
---------------------------------------------
   S1           1.000   1.000   1.000
```

The printed output for intermediate solutions contains an additional line between the header and the solution part for that minimal sum of the parsimonious solution p.sol from which the intermediate solution has been derived. This implies that if rowdom had been set to FALSE, there would have been two intermediate solutions.

Sometimes it is desired that common literals across different PIs be emphasized in solutions. For this purpose, minimal sums can be factorized using QCA's factorize() function.

```
> factorize(KrookSI)

    p.sol: WS + ES*WM + QU*LP + WM*LP

S: ES*WS + WM*LP + ES*QU*LP + ES*QU*WM

F1: ES*QU*(LP + WM) + ES*WS + WM*LP
F2: WM*(LP + ES*QU) + ES*(WS + QU*LP)
F3: LP*(WM + ES*QU) + ES*(WS + QU*WM)
F4: ES*(WS + QU*LP + QU*WM) + WM*LP
```

There exist four possible factorizations of the intermediate solution. The one which best underlines the theoretical argument to be made in the analysis should ideally be chosen. If the importance of **ES** is to be stressed, F_4 provides a suitable representation of the solution.

The defining characteristic of intermediate solutions is that SAs are filtered according to a set of "rules" formulated by the researcher. In order to provide maximum flexibility in formulating these rules, it is also possible in QCA to impose any kind of further restriction on the minimization procedure by excluding specific logical remainders. Individual exclusions can be achieved by means of the omit argument. For example, if the parsimonious solution should be generated, but without making potential use of those remainder configurations as SAs which have only one condition present at most, omit requires a vector of those truth table row names that correspond to these remainders. With truth tables of low dimensions, these rows can easily be found by visual inspection of the complete truth table.[22] Rows 1, 2, 5, and 17 have only one condition present at most.[23]

```
> KrookSR <- eqmcc(KrookTT, include = "?", omit = c(1,2,5,17),
+   details = TRUE)
> KrookSR

n OUT = 1/0/C: 11/11/0
  Total      : 22

S1: ES*WM + ES*WS + QU*LP + WM*LP
```

---

[22] Call up KrookTT again or scroll back in the R console.

[23] The omit argument always converts a numeric vector to a character vector of row names.

		incl	PRI	cov.r	cov.u
1	ES*WM	1.000	1.000	0.545	0.091
2	ES*WS	1.000	1.000	0.455	0.182
3	QU*LP	1.000	1.000	0.545	0.091
4	WM*LP	1.000	1.000	0.636	0.091
	S1	1.000	1.000	1.000	

With truth tables of higher dimensions, visual inspection becomes error-prone. The rows to be omitted should therefore be collected by means of automated methods. For example, the above result could also be achieved by first calculating the row sums of all configurations with R's rowSums() function, and then extracting those elements that are both remainders and have a value below two. The which() function and the logical & operator are suitable for this purpose. The row sum should be lower than two, and not equal to one because those configurations are sought which have one condition present at most. Just as all objects returned by eqmcc() have various components, so have all objects returned by truthTable(). One of them, the tt component, has already been introduced above. It contains the actual truth table. The conditions are the first five columns, over which the row sum is to be formed. Finally, the names() function extracts the wanted row names.

```
> sums <- rowSums(KrookTT$tt[, 1:5])
> omRows <- which(KrookTT$tt$OUT == "?" & sums < 2)
> (omRows <- names(omRows))

[1] "1"  "2"  "5"  "17"
```

The vector omRows could then be passed directly to the omit argument in eqmcc().

3.3.4.3 Contradictory Simplifying Assumptions

Contradictory simplifying assumptions (CSA) are logical remainders which enter into the derivation of the solution with respect to the outcome set as well as its negation. Reconsider the second minimal sum of the parsimonious solution, S_2: WS + ES · WM + QU · LP + WM · LP. First, the minimization has to be carried out for the negation of the outcome. As neither the truth table nor the solution details are of immediate interest here, the eqmcc() function can be called directly on the original dataset instead of the truth table. If the object passed to eqmcc() is not a truth table object but a data frame or matrix of set data, the logical argument neg.out negates the outcome.[24]

---

[24] If a truth table object is passed to eqmcc(), the neg.out argument has no effect.

```
> KrookSPn <- eqmcc(Krook, outcome = "WNP", neg.out = TRUE,
+   include = "?")
> KrookSPn

S1: es*lp + ws*wm*lp + (ES*qu*ws)
S2: es*lp + ws*wm*lp + (qu*wm*LP)
S3: es*lp + ws*wm*lp + (qu*ws*wm)
```

The parsimonious solution for the negation of the outcome set consists of three
minimal sums, none of which dominates any other.[25] We thus choose all three minimal sums here in testing for CSAs. How to access SAs has been shown above in
Sect. 3.3.4.1. First, three vectors of those truth table row names are generated which
identify the respective SAs for each minimal sum. They can be extracted with the
rownames() function.

```
> (SAs1n <- rownames(KrookSPn$SA$S1))

[1] "1"  "5"  "7"  "13" "15" "17" "19" "20"

> (SAs2n <- rownames(KrookSPn$SA$S2))

[1] "1"  "2"  "5"  "6"  "7"  "13" "15" "17" "22"

> (SAs3n <- rownames(KrookSPn$SA$S3))

[1] "1"  "2"  "5"  "7"  "13" "15" "17"
```

Second, we need the SAs for minimal sum S_2 from the original analysis performed
in Sect. 3.3.4.1.

```
> (SAs2 <- rownames(KrookSP$SA$S2))

 [1] "5"  "6"  "7"  "8"  "10" "13" "14" "15" "16" "19" "20"
[12] "22" "23" "30" "31"
```

With only relatively few SAs, visual inspection may be sufficient. However, it
is always better to apply a formal test, in particular when the numbers of SAs
become larger. Most suitably, the intersect() function introduced in Sect. 2.9
can be employed to test whether there exist any shared SAs.

```
> (CSA1 <- intersect(SAs1n, SAs2))

[1] "5"  "7"  "13" "15" "19" "20"

> (CSA2 <- intersect(SAs2n, SAs2))

[1] "5"  "6"  "7"  "13" "15" "22"
```

---

[25] Note that the same solution would have resulted had the minimization been run on all false
configurations in the original truth table. However, this mirror relation does not always hold.

```
> (CSA3 <- intersect(SAs3n, SAs2))
[1] "5"   "7"   "13" "15"
```

The intersections of the SAs for each minimal sum of the solution for the negated outcome set and the SAs for minimal sum S_2 of the original solution contain different logical remainders. Those logical remainders that appear in all these intersections can be found by applying the intersect() function twice in a nested structure.

```
> (CSAall <- intersect(intersect(CSA1, CSA2), CSA3))
[1] "5"   "7"   "13" "15"
```

Four logical remainders are common to all combinations of the minimal sums. By using the character vector CSAall to index the truth table component of KrookTT, the exact configurations can be found.

```
> KrookTT$tt[CSAall, ]
```

	ES	QU	WS	WM	LP	OUT	n	incl	PRI
5	0	0	1	0	0	?	0	-	-
7	0	0	1	1	0	?	0	-	-
13	0	1	1	0	0	?	0	-	-
15	0	1	1	1	0	?	0	-	-

3.3.5 Plotting Results

In Sect. 3.2.3, it was shown how to use VennDiagram's venn.diagram() function to visualize results in csQCA. As the VennDiagram package only supports diagrams of order four, we only demonstrate how to plot the first three PIs from the intermediate solution generated in Sect. 3.3.4.2.[26]

Similar to the coms component in objects returned by superSubset(), eqmcc() returns a pims component, which contains all PI membership scores. As it is the intermediate solution for which these scores are required, the relevant subcomponent of pims is i.sol. The last piece of information that is needed concerns the respective complex and parsimonious solution from which the intermediate solution has been formed. The row dominance principle has been applied in the derivation of KrookSI, and we know that the parsimonious solution only contains one minimal sum. As intermediate solutions always result from a unique combination of a minimal sum from the complex solution and one from the parsimonious solution, the identifier in the solution subcomponent of pims indexes the respective combination. In our example, the combination of the first (and only) minimal sum from the complex solution and the first (and only) minimal sum from the parsimonious solution is therefore indexed by C1P1.

---

[26] The authors of the VennDiagram package argue that Venn diagrams become too complex for intuitive visualization with more sets (Chen and Boutros 2011, p. 37).

Fig. 3.6 Venn diagram of
intermediate solution PIs in
csQCA

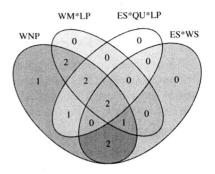

```
> PIms <- KrookSI$pims$i.sol$C1P1
> PIms[ , 1:3]

   ES*WS WM*LP ES*QU*LP
SE    1     0       0
FI    1     0       0
NO    1     1       1
..    .     .       .
<<rest omitted>>
```

The code for producing the Venn diagram shown in Fig. 3.6 has exactly the same
structure as that used for generating Fig. 3.3. The only difference is that the object
with the combination membership scores COms has been replaced with the object
containing the PI membership scores PIms.

```
> vennKrookSuf <- venn.diagram(
+   x = list(
+     "WNP" = which(Krook$WNP == 1),
+     "ES*WS" = which(PIms[ , 1] == 1),
+     "WM*LP" = which(PIms[ , 2] == 1),
+     "ES*QU*LP" = which(PIms[ , 3] == 1)),
+   filename = NULL,
+   cex = 2.5, cat.cex = 2, cat.pos = c(350, 10, 0, 0),
+   cat.dist = c(0.22, 0.22, 0.12, 0.12),
+   fill = gray(c(0.3, 0.5, 0.7, 0.9))
+ )
> grid.draw(vennKrookSuf)
```

Chapter 4
Fuzzy-Set QCA

Abstract This section explains how to perform QCA using fuzzy sets, commonly referred to as fsQCA. Since the publication of Ragin (2000), fsQCA has become increasingly popular because continuous base variables need not be dichotomized. After a short theoretical introduction to the concept of fuzzy-set calibration, we introduce the two most popular calibration methods: direct assignment and transformational assignment. While the former is quickly dealt with, more time will be spent on the latter as its mechanisms and implications have so far received little attention. In the remainder of the chapter, the results from the study by Emmenegger (2011) on job-security regulations in Western democracies are replicated.

4.1 Calibrating Fuzzy Sets

The process of getting from base variable values (also called *raw data*) to condition or outcome set membership scores is generally referred to as *calibration*, in fsQCA often also as *fuzzification*. Applications of fsQCA in most areas of the social sciences make use of two different calibration procedures. The first is the method of *direct assignment*, whereby fuzzy-set membership scores are derived from base variable values solely through the researcher's or another expert's judgement. The second is the method of *transformational assignment*, whereby base variable values are mapped into the unit interval with the help of continuous functions for which only minimal information is provided by the researcher. The essential difference between direct and transformational assignments therefore builds on the same difference that exists between discrete and continuous random variables in statistics. More space in this section has been allocated to transformational assignments because this procedure has been devoted much less attention in applications of and methodological studies about fsQCA. In this connection, some theoretical preliminaries are necessary in order to fully understand the implementation of fuzzy-set calibration methods in the QCA package.

A. Thiem and A. Duşa, *Qualitative Comparative Analysis with R*,
SpringerBriefs in Political Science, DOI: 10.1007/978-1-4614-4584-5_4,

4.1.1 Theoretical Preliminaries

In order to fully understand the practicalities of calibrating fuzzy sets, it is important to first delve a little into the theory behind it. Essentially, sets represent concepts comprising multiple levels, two most fundamental of which are what Goertz (2006) refers to as the "basic level" and the "indicator level." The indicator level captures the *kind* of the concept, and the *degree* to which some observation corresponds to that kind is measured on the indicator level. In order to provide a taxonomy of calibration scenarios, we link these two levels across two *concept types*, each with two specific *concept type relations*. These concept type relations cover the vast majority of calibration scenarios which may occur in social science research.

The two concept types shall be referred to as *end-point concept* and *mid-point concept*. End-point concepts are of a positive relation when set membership scores do not decrease with increasing values on the base variable, but usually increase. In contrast, end-point concepts are of a negative relation when set membership scores do not increase with increasing values on the base variable, but usually decrease.[1] As a fuzzy set is tied in degree and kind to its base variable, this tie determines whether an end-point concept is positive or negative. A number of examples are to be given in the following to clarify these relations.

First, consider the set of "non-democratic countries." There exists a whole raft of potential base variables in the comparative politics literature from which this set could be calibrated (Coppedge et al. 2011; Munck and Verkuilen 2002). The "Freedom in the World" country ratings published by Freedom House (Freedom-House index (FHI)) is one of them. It ranges from 1 to 7 at increments of 0.5, with higher scores indicating less democracy.[2] If this index is chosen as the base variable, then the form of the membership function must reflect a positive end-point concept. As the value of a country under the base variable increases, so does its membership score in the set of "non-democratic countries." Conversely, the set of "democratic countries" represents a negative end-point concept if tied to the FHI. As its value on the index increases, a country's membership score in this set decreases.

Sets based on end-point concept are therefore characterized by extreme membership scores towards both ends of the empirical range of their underlying base variable. Sets based on a mid-point concept type also have extreme membership scores along that range. However, in contrast to end-point concepts, mid-point concepts exhibit identical extremes towards either end of the empirical range of their underlying base variable, and another extreme between them. As with end-point concepts, they can also be positive or negative, depending on the way in which they are linked to their base variables. Mid-point concepts are positive when set membership scores first

---

[1] There can be some interval on the base variable $[x_i, x_j]$ over which set membership scores remain equal, but it is generally assumed that they vary over some interval along the domain, usually between the threshold for set exclusion and that for set inclusion.

[2] More precisely, the Freedom House index measures freedom rather than democracy, but its two dimensions include political rights and civil liberties. For more details about the data and documentation, see http://www.freedomhouse.org.

Table 4.1 Concept types and their relations

Concept Type		
End-point	*base variable*: Freedom-House index *target set*: non-democratic countries	*base variable*: Freedom-House index *target set*: democratic countries
Mid-point	*base variable*: Herfindahl index *target set*: oligopolistic markets	*base variable*: Herfindahl index *target set*: non-oligopolistic markets
	Positive	Negative
	Concept Type Relation	

increase with increasing values on the base variable, and decrease thereafter. They are negative when set membership scores first decrease with increasing values on the base variable, and increase thereafter. From this perspective, mid-point concepts can thus be conceived of as two end-point concepts (positive and negative) with a bifurcated base variable that have been joined together. An illustrative example from the field of economics is the set of "oligopolistic markets."

Oligopolies are market structures between the extremes of perfect competition, where many firms provide the same or a very similar product, and monopoly with only one firm. If fuzzification is based on the Herfindahl–Hirschman index, with values close to 1 indicating monopolies and values close to 0 indicating perfect competition, then there exists a certain point to either of whose sides a case's membership in the set of oligopolistic market structures will decrease.[3] In consequence, the mid-point concept is positive because going from perfect competition to monopoly on the index means first increasing membership scores up to oligopoly, then decreasing membership scores up to monopoly. By analogy, the set of "non-oligopolistic market structures" using the Herfindahl–Hirschman index is a negative mid-point concept.[4] The two concept types introduced above and the two relations they can assume are summarized in Table 4.1.

---

[3] The Herfindahl–Hirschman index measures the size of firms in relation to their industry and thus indicates the degree of competition between them. Different versions of this index exist.

[4] Another example of a set based on a mid-point concept is the set of "moderately developed countries". The example given in Table 5.3, Ragin (2008, p. 93), claims to demonstrate the calibration of the set of "moderately developed countries", whereas in fact it describes the calibration of the set of "at least moderately developed countries" as written in the text. The former is a mid-point concept and must be calibrated by a different function from that applied to calibrate the latter.

4.1.2 Direct Assignment

With the method of direct assignment, fuzzy-set membership scores are directly
arrived at through expert knowledge (Verkuilen 2005). For demonstrative purposes,
we simulate our own dataset of FHI scores for 30 countries. The index ranges from
1 to 7 at increments of 0.5, with lower scores representing more democracy. The
sample() function introduced in Sect. 2.9 can be used to generate a number of
random draws, passing it a sequence of index scores that consists of all possible index
values. Its optional argument replace must be set to TRUE because the number of
draws (30) exceeds the number of possible values (13). For a better overview, the
sort() function is used to order the values from smallest to largest.

```
> set.seed(10)
> fhi <- sample(seq(1, 7, 0.5), 30, replace = TRUE)
> fhi <- sort(fhi)
> fhi

 [1] 1.0 1.5 1.5 2.0 2.5 2.5 2.5 2.5 2.5 3.0 3.0 3.0 3.5 3.5
[15] 3.5 3.5 3.5 4.0 4.5 4.5 4.5 5.0 5.0 5.5 5.5 6.0 6.0 6.0
[29] 6.0 6.5
```

Suppose the base variable fhi should now be fuzzified into three categories in
order to construct the set of "non-democratic countries," denoted by lower case **dem**:
0.33 for "democratic," 0.66 for "partly democratic" and 1 for "non-democratic." As
already shown for the calibration of crisp sets in Sect. 3.1, the ifelse() function
offers an efficient solution. Recall that it has three elements: a test, a value if the test
returns true, and a value if the test returns false. Instead of specifying a particular
value if the test returns false, however, we can as well perform a new test. The
nesting of sequential tests can be expanded until all desired categories of fuzzy-set
membership scores have been covered. In our case, two tests suffice. The researcher
decides—based on theoretical and/or empirical knowledge—that a membership of
0.33 in **dem** should be assigned to cases whose index value falls in the interval
[1.0, 2.5), 0.66 if in [2.5, 5.0) and 1 otherwise.[5]

```
> dem <- ifelse(1.0 <= fhi & fhi < 2.5, 0.33,
+          ifelse(2.5 <= fhi & fhi < 5.0, 0.66,
+          1))
> dem

 [1] 0.33 0.33 0.33 0.33 0.66 0.66 0.66 0.66 0.66 0.66 0.66
[12] 0.66 0.66 0.66 0.66 0.66 0.66 0.66 0.66 0.66 0.66 1.00
[23] 1.00 1.00 1.00 1.00 1.00 1.00 1.00 1.00
```

While direct assignments only require a simple recoding of the data from continuous base variables into a small number of membership score categories, transformational assignments are more taxing in that the researcher has to first decide

---

[5] Square brackets mean "inclusive of," round brackets "exclusive of".

on a suitable membership function for recoding a continuous base variable into a continuous fuzzy set.

4.1.3 Transformational Assignment

In fsQCA, continuous base variables need not be categorized by the researcher, but they can also be transformed into fuzzy-set membership scores with the help of continuous functions. Ragin (2008), for example, calls this procedure the *direct method*, which makes use of a piecewise logistic function. Other authors refer to it more generally as *assignment by transformation* (Verkuilen 2005, p. 465). We adopt the latter terminology here because the word "direct" is often associated with the calibration method of direct assignment. In addition, transformational assignments are not associated with any functional form in particular, whereas Ragin's direct method explicitly uses only the piecewise logistic.

Some baseline choices for transformational assignments exist, but potentially, any function which possesses the properties desired by the analyst could be used (Thiem 2010).[6] Decisions for or against specific functions, however, may have consequential downstream effects. It is therefore incumbent on the researcher to control the calibration process by carefully considering the form of the membership function. At the very least, this form is determined by the nature of the concept underlying the set and its base variable.[7]

For calibrating sets based on positive end-point concepts, Eq. (4.1) is implemented in QCA.

$$\mu_{\mathbf{SET}}(x, \tau_{[...]}, p, q) = \begin{cases} 0 & \text{if } \tau_{ex} \geq x_i, \\ \frac{1}{2}\left(\frac{\tau_{ex}-x_i}{\tau_{ex}-\tau_{cr}}\right)^p & \text{if } \tau_{ex} < x_i \leq \tau_{cr}, \\ 1 - \frac{1}{2}\left(\frac{\tau_{in}-x_i}{\tau_{in}-\tau_{cr}}\right)^q & \text{if } \tau_{cr} < x_i \leq \tau_{in}, \\ 1 & \text{if } \tau_{in} < x_i. \end{cases} \qquad (4.1)$$

where x denotes the base variable, τ_{ex} the threshold for full exclusion from **SET**, τ_{cr} the crossover threshold at the point of maximally ambiguous set membership in **SET**, τ_{in} the threshold for full inclusion in **SET**, and p as well as q are parameters for controlling the degrees of concentration and dilation.

For calibrating sets based on negative end-point concepts, Eq. (4.2) is implemented in QCA.

---

[6] Only the piecewise logistic function is available in fs/QCA through the "calibrate" command and in the QCA3 package through the directCalibration() command. Both functions differ slightly from each other.

[7] By "form of the membership function," we mean both the choice of the calibration thresholds and the membership function.

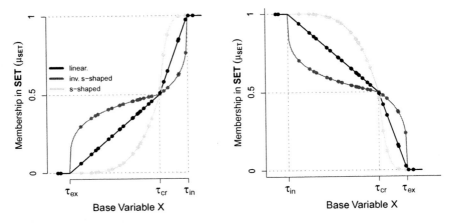

Fig. 4.1 Positive (*left*) and Negative (*right*) end-point concepts

$$\mu_{\text{SET}}(x, \tau_{[\dots]}, p, q) = \begin{cases} 1 & \text{if } \tau_{\text{in}} \geq x_i, \\ 1 - \frac{1}{2}\left(\frac{\tau_{\text{in}} - x_i}{\tau_{\text{in}} - \tau_{\text{cr}}}\right)^q & \text{if } \tau_{\text{in}} < x_i \leq \tau_{\text{cr}}, \\ \frac{1}{2}\left(\frac{\tau_{\text{ex}} - x_i}{\tau_{\text{ex}} - \tau_{\text{cr}}}\right)^p & \text{if } \tau_{\text{cr}} < x_i \leq \tau_{\text{ex}}, \\ 0 & \text{if } \tau_{\text{ex}} < x_i. \end{cases} \quad (4.2)$$

The denotation is analogous to that for Eq. (4.1). By adjusting p and q accordingly, both functions can accommodate linear, s-shaped, and inverted s-shaped relations as special cases (Clark et al. 2008, pp. 37–45; Bojadziev and Bojadziev 2007, pp. 19–26). One example of each such relation is pictured in Fig. 4.1, for positive end-point concepts in the left panel and negative end-point concepts in the right panel. Linear membership functions (black) result for $p = q = 1$, s-shaped membership functions (light-gray) for $p > 1$ and $q > 1$, and inverted s-shaped membership functions (gray) for $0 < p < 1$ and $0 < q < 1$.[8]

For calibrating sets based on positive mid-point concepts, Eq. (4.3) is implemented in QCA.

$$\mu_{\text{SET}}(x, \tau_{[\dots]}, p, q) = \begin{cases} 0 & \text{if } \tau_{\text{ex}1} \geq x_i, \\ \frac{1}{2}\left(\frac{\tau_{\text{ex}1} - x_i}{\tau_{\text{ex}1} - \tau_{\text{cr}1}}\right)^p & \text{if } \tau_{\text{ex}1} < x_i \leq \tau_{\text{cr}1}, \\ 1 - \frac{1}{2}\left(\frac{\tau_{\text{in}1} - x_i}{\tau_{\text{in}1} - \tau_{\text{cr}1}}\right)^q & \text{if } \tau_{\text{cr}1} < x_i < \tau_{\text{in}1}, \\ 1 & \text{if } \tau_{\text{in}1} \leq x_i \leq \tau_{\text{in}2}, \\ 1 - \frac{1}{2}\left(\frac{\tau_{\text{in}2} - x_i}{\tau_{\text{in}2} - \tau_{\text{cr}2}}\right)^q & \text{if } \tau_{\text{in}2} < x_i \leq \tau_{\text{cr}2}, \\ \frac{1}{2}\left(\frac{\tau_{\text{ex}2} - x_i}{\tau_{\text{ex}2} - \tau_{\text{cr}2}}\right)^p & \text{if } \tau_{\text{cr}2} < x_i \leq \tau_{\text{ex}2}, \\ 0 & \text{if } \tau_{\text{ex}2} < x_i. \end{cases} \quad (4.3)$$

---

[8] It is possible to combine $p > 1$ and $0 < q < 1$, $0 < p < 1$ and $q > 1$ respectively, to get double-concentrated or double-dilated membership functions.

where x denotes the base variable, $\tau_{\text{ex}1}$ the first (left) threshold for full exclusion from **SET**, $\tau_{\text{cr}1}$ the first (left) crossover threshold, $\tau_{\text{in}1}$ the first (left) threshold for full inclusion in **SET**, $\tau_{\text{in}2}$ the second (right) threshold for full inclusion in **SET**, $\tau_{\text{cr}2}$ the second (right) crossover threshold, $\tau_{\text{ex}2}$ the second (right) threshold for full exclusion from **SET**, and p as well as q are again parameters for controlling the degrees of concentration and dilation.

For calibrating sets based on negative mid-point concepts, Eq. (4.4) is implemented in QCA.

$$\mu_{\textbf{SET}}(x, \tau_{[\dots]}, p, q) = \begin{cases} 1 & \text{if } \tau_{\text{in}1} \geq x_i, \\ 1 - \frac{1}{2}\left(\frac{\tau_{\text{in}1} - x_i}{\tau_{\text{in}1} - \tau_{\text{cr}1}}\right)^q & \text{if } \tau_{\text{in}1} < x_i \leq \tau_{\text{cr}1}, \\ \frac{1}{2}\left(\frac{\tau_{\text{ex}1} - x_i}{\tau_{\text{ex}1} - \tau_{\text{cr}1}}\right)^p & \text{if } \tau_{\text{cr}1} < x_i < \tau_{\text{ex}1}, \\ 0 & \text{if } \tau_{\text{ex}1} \leq x_i \leq \tau_{\text{ex}2}, \\ \frac{1}{2}\left(\frac{\tau_{\text{ex}2} - x_i}{\tau_{\text{ex}2} - \tau_{\text{cr}2}}\right)^p & \text{if } \tau_{\text{ex}2} < x_i \leq \tau_{\text{cr}2}, \\ 1 - \frac{1}{2}\left(\frac{\tau_{\text{in}2} - x_i}{\tau_{\text{in}2} - \tau_{\text{cr}2}}\right)^q & \text{if } \tau_{\text{cr}2} < x_i \leq \tau_{\text{in}2}, \\ 1 & \text{if } \tau_{\text{in}2} < x_i. \end{cases} \quad (4.4)$$

The denotation is analogous to that for Eq. (4.1). By adjusting p and q accordingly, both functions can accommodate trapezoidal, triangular, and bell-shaped relations as special cases (Clark et al. 2008, pp. 37–45; Bojadziev and Bojadziev 2007, pp. 19–26). One example of each such relation is pictured in Fig. 4.2, for positive mid-point concepts in the left panel and negative mid-point concepts in the right panel. Triangular membership functions (black) for positive mid-point concepts result when $p = q = 1$ and $\tau_{\text{in}1} = \tau_{\text{in}2}$, for negative mid-point concepts when $p = q = 1$ and $\tau_{\text{ex}1} = \tau_{\text{ex}2}$. Trapezoidal membership functions (light-gray) for positive mid-point concepts result when $p = q = 1$ and $\tau_{\text{in}1} \neq \tau_{\text{in}2}$, for negative mid-point concepts when $p = q = 1$ and $\tau_{\text{ex}1} \neq \tau_{\text{ex}2}$. Bell-shaped membership functions (gray) result when $p > 1$ and $q > 1$. An example for an inverted bell-shaped membership function is not shown in Fig. 4.2. It results when $0 < p < 1$ and $0 < q < 1$.

Just as with the calibration of crisp sets, the calibration of fuzzy sets is achieved in QCA with the `calibrate()` function. For fuzzification, it takes three mandatory arguments: the base variable to be transformed, the information that the target set is fuzzy, and a numeric vector of thresholds. Three thresholds must be provided in the case of end-point concepts: the threshold for full set exclusion τ_{ex}, the threshold for the set crossover τ_{cr}, and the threshold for full set inclusion τ_{in}. This order of thresholds must be adhered to, but the user need not specify whether the target set is based on a positive or a negative end-point concept. The `calibrate()` function will automatically recognize which of the two is the case. It will apply Eq. (4.1) if $\tau_{\text{ex}} < \tau_{\text{cr}} < \tau_{\text{in}}$ and Eq. (4.2) if $\tau_{\text{in}} < \tau_{\text{cr}} < \tau_{\text{ex}}$. Equalities of thresholds are not allowed because two cases with the same value on the base variable cannot be members of the same target set to different degrees, whereas they can be members of a set to the same degree with different values on the associated base variable.

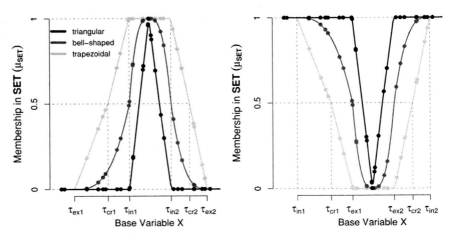

Fig. 4.2 Positive (*left panel*) and negative (*right panel*) mid-point concepts

Assume that for calibrating the set of "non-democratic countries"—let it be denoted by **dem** again—the following thresholds are established: 2 for full exclusion, 4 for maximally ambiguous set membership, and 6 for full inclusion. We reuse the example of FHI values from Sect. 4.1.2.

Full syntax:

```
> dem <- calibrate(fhi, type = "fuzzy",
+   thresholds = c(2, 4, 6), include = TRUE, logistic = FALSE,
+   idm = 0.95, ecdf = FALSE, p = 1, q = 1)
```

```
> dem <- calibrate(fhi, type = "fuzzy",
+   thresholds = c(2, 4, 6))
> round(dem, 2)

 [1] 0.00 0.00 0.00 0.00 0.12 0.12 0.12 0.12 0.12 0.25 0.25
[12] 0.25 0.38 0.38 0.38 0.38 0.38 0.50 0.62 0.62 0.62 0.75
[23] 0.75 0.88 0.88 1.00 1.00 1.00 1.00 1.00
```

After the base variable fhi, the `type` argument specifies the nature of the target set and the `thresholds` argument the three thresholds in the following order: τ_{ex}, τ_{cr} and τ_{in}.

Now assume that for calibrating the set of "democratic countries"—**DEM**—the following thresholds are established: 6 for full exclusion, 4 for maximally ambiguous set membership, and 2 for full inclusion.

```
> DEM <- calibrate(fhi, type = "fuzzy",
+   thresholds = c(6, 4, 2))
> round(DEM, 2)

 [1] 1.00 1.00 1.00 1.00 0.88 0.88 0.88 0.88 0.88 0.75 0.75
[12] 0.75 0.62 0.62 0.62 0.62 0.62 0.50 0.38 0.38 0.38 0.25
[23] 0.25 0.12 0.12 0.00 0.00 0.00 0.00 0.00
```

As the order of thresholds is fixed, the `calibrate()` function recognizes that the target set must be based on a negative end-point concept. Since the same thresholds are applied as for the construction of **dem**, **dem + DEM** = 1.

In the case of mid-point concepts, six thresholds must be provided: the first (left) threshold for full set exclusion τ_{ex1}, the first (left) threshold for the set crossover τ_{cr1}, the first (left) threshold for full set inclusion τ_{in1}, the second (right) threshold for full set inclusion τ_{in2}, the second (right) threshold for the set crossover τ_{cr2} and the second (right) threshold for full set exclusion τ_{ex2}. This order of thresholds must be adhered to, but the user need not specify whether the target set is based on a positive or a negative mid-point concept. The `calibrate()` function will automatically recognize which of the two is the case. It will apply Eq. (4.3) if $\tau_{ex1} < \tau_{cr1} < \tau_{in1} \leq \tau_{in2} < \tau_{cr2} < \tau_{ex2}$ and Eq. (4.4) if $\tau_{in1} < \tau_{cr1} < \tau_{ex1} \leq \tau_{ex2} < \tau_{cr2} < \tau_{in2}$. Equalities of thresholds other than $\tau_{in1} = \tau_{in2}$ for positive mid-point concepts and $\tau_{ex1} = \tau_{ex2}$ for negative mid-point concepts are not allowed for the same reason given above in relation to end-point concepts.

Assume that for calibrating the set of "partly democratic countries"—let it be denoted by **PTDEM**—the following thresholds are established: 2 and 6 for full exclusion, 3 and 5 for maximally ambiguous set membership, and 4 for full inclusion. The six thresholds must be provided in the following order: τ_{ex1}, τ_{cr1}, τ_{in1}, τ_{in2}, τ_{cr2} and τ_{ex2}.

```
> PTDEM <- calibrate(fhi, type = "fuzzy",
+   thresholds = c(2, 3, 4, 4, 5, 6))
> round(PTDEM, 2)

 [1] 0.00 0.00 0.00 0.00 0.25 0.25 0.25 0.25 0.25 0.50 0.50
[12] 0.50 0.75 0.75 0.75 0.75 0.75 1.00 0.75 0.75 0.75 0.50
[23] 0.50 0.25 0.25 0.00 0.00 0.00 0.00 0.00
```

Now assume that for calibrating the set of "not partly democratic countries"—let it be denoted by **ptdem**—the following thresholds are established: 2 and 6 for full inclusion, 3 and 5 for maximally ambiguous set membership, and 4 for full exclusion.

```
> ptdem <- calibrate(fhi, type = "fuzzy",
+   thresholds = c(4, 3, 2, 6, 5, 4))
> round(ptdem, 2)

 [1] 1.00 1.00 1.00 1.00 0.75 0.75 0.75 0.75 0.75 0.50 0.50
[12] 0.50 0.25 0.25 0.25 0.25 0.25 0.00 0.25 0.25 0.25 0.50
[23] 0.50 0.75 0.75 1.00 1.00 1.00 1.00 1.00
```

As the order of thresholds is fixed, `calibrate()` recognizes that the target set must be based on a negative mid-point concept. Since the same thresholds are applied as for the construction of **PTDEM, ptdem** $= 1 -$ **PTDEM**.

In addition to Eqs. (4.1)–(4.4), `calibrate()` is also capable of applying the piecewise logistic function, both with negative and positive end-point concepts. The procedure is essentially the same as the one described by Ragin (2008, pp. 89–94), but the formula implemented in **QCA** differs insofar as it applies exact logged odds for the degrees of membership chosen by the user to represent full inclusion in the target set and full exclusion from it. The formula for the piecewise logistic is given in Eq. (4.5).

$$
\mu_{\mathrm{SET}}(x, \tau_{[\ldots]}, \phi) =
\begin{cases}
1/\left(1 + e^{-\left[(x_i - \tau_{\mathrm{cr}})\left(\frac{-\phi}{\tau_{\mathrm{ex}} - \tau_{\mathrm{cr}}}\right)\right]}\right) & \text{if } x_i < \tau_{\mathrm{cr}}, \\
1/\left(1 + e^{-\left[(x_i - \tau_{\mathrm{cr}})\left(\frac{\phi}{\tau_{\mathrm{in}} - \tau_{\mathrm{cr}}}\right)\right]}\right) & \text{if } x_i \geq \tau_{\mathrm{cr}}.
\end{cases}
\tag{4.5}
$$

The parameter ϕ denotes the logged odds of the degree of membership the user specifies for full set inclusion. As Eq. (4.5) is symmetric around the logged odds of the crossover, the user need not specify the degree of membership for full set exclusion in addition. By providing the argument `logistic = TRUE` to `calibrate()`, the logistic function can be invoked. The calibration of the set of "democratic countries"— call it **LOGDEM** now to emphasize the use of the logistic function—with the same thresholds is achieved as follows.

```
> LOGDEM <- calibrate(fhi, type = "fuzzy",
+   thresholds = c(6, 4, 2), logistic = TRUE, idm = 0.99)
> round(LOGDEM, 2)

 [1]  1.00 1.00 1.00 0.99 0.97 0.97 0.97 0.97 0.97 0.91 0.91
[12]  0.91 0.76 0.76 0.76 0.76 0.76 0.50 0.24 0.24 0.24 0.09
[23]  0.09 0.03 0.03 0.01 0.01 0.01 0.01 0.00
```

The argument `idm` specifies the inclusion degree of membership. Its default is 0.95 as shown in (Ragin 2008, pp. 89ff.), but here it has been set to 0.99 for demonstration purposes.[9] All membership scores assigned through the logistic in this way, except that for the crossover threshold, will almost always differ from those assigned through Eqs. (4.1), (4.2) respectively. Even small differences in assigned membership scores may change final solutions, so the researcher should analyze what effects the application of different membership functions has.[10] As a general guideline, we recommend beginning with the standard settings in the `calibrate()` function if no theoretical or empirical reasons for changing them exist.

---

[9] A value of 0.95 requires $\phi = \log(19)$, 0.975 $\phi = \log(39)$, 0.98 $\phi = \log(49)$, 0.99 $\phi = \log(99)$, and so on.

[10] The arbitrariness of membership functions has been one of the main criticisms in fuzzy-set theory (Arfi 2010, pp. 5f.).

In some cases, a fuzzification procedure that is based on the empirical distribution of base variable values, and not on some theoretical membership function that imposes an artificial continuity on the transformation process, may be preferred. To this end, `calibrate()` also provides a calibration solution that is based on the empirical cumulative distribution function (ECDF) of the base variable. Its formula is given in Eq. (4.6).

$$
\mu_{\text{SET}}(x, \tau_{[\ldots]}) = \begin{cases} 0 & \text{if } \tau_{\text{ex}} \geq x_i, \\ \frac{1}{2} \frac{F(x_i)}{F(\tau_{\text{cr}})} & \text{if } \tau_{\text{ex}} < x_i \leq \tau_{\text{cr}}, \\ 1 - \frac{1}{2} \left(\frac{1-F(x_i)}{1-F(\tau_{\text{cr}})} \right) & \text{if } \tau_{\text{cr}} < x_i \leq \tau_{\text{in}}, \\ 1 & \text{if } \tau_{\text{in}} < x_i. \end{cases} \tag{4.6}
$$

More precisely, Eq. (4.6) applies a double-truncated ECDF, which combines the qualitative information provided by the researcher through the specification of thresholds with valuable information contained in the base variable. That membership functions should resemble the concept in hand as closely as possible has been given as a general advice in the literature (Kvist 2006, p. 174), and ECDFs often come closer to fulfilling this requirement than the solutions presented above. The social meaning of a concept often arises from the contemporary distribution of values under its indicator variable. For example, as more people become rich, the meaning of richness as a social-scientific concept changes accordingly. The strategy of identifying membership functions by means of base variable characteristics thus increases in attractiveness with the extent to which the cases used in the analysis are representative of or even identical with their respective unit space under this particular variable.

For example, the fuzzification of the set of "democratic countries"—call it **CDFDEM** to emphasize the use of the (E)CDF—can be achieved as follows.

```
> CDFDEM <- calibrate(fhi, type = "fuzzy",
+   thresholds = c(6, 4, 2), ecdf = TRUE)
> round(CDFDEM, 2)

 [1] 1.00 1.00 1.00 1.00 0.80 0.80 0.80 0.80 0.80 0.70 0.70
[12] 0.70 0.53 0.53 0.53 0.53 0.53 0.50 0.36 0.36 0.36 0.27
[23] 0.27 0.18 0.18 0.00 0.00 0.00 0.00 0.00
```

$$
\mu_{\text{SET}}(x, \tau_{[\ldots]}) = \begin{cases} 1 & \text{if } \tau_{\text{in}} \geq x_i, \\ 1 - \frac{1}{2} \frac{F(x_i)}{F(\tau_{\text{cr}})} & \text{if } \tau_{\text{in}} < x_i \leq \tau_{\text{cr}}, \\ \frac{1}{2} \left(\frac{1-F(x_i)}{1-F(\tau_{\text{cr}})} \right) & \text{if } \tau_{\text{cr}} < x_i \leq \tau_{\text{ex}}, \\ 0 & \text{if } \tau_{\text{ex}} < x_i. \end{cases} \tag{4.7}
$$

Accordingly, the fuzzification of the set of "non-democratic countries" **cdfdem** draws on Eq. (4.7) and only requires the thresholds to be reversed.

```
> ecdfdem <- calibrate(fhi, type = "fuzzy",
+  thresholds = c(2, 4, 6), ecdf = TRUE)
> round(ecdfdem, 2)

 [1] 0.00 0.00 0.00 0.00 0.20 0.20 0.20 0.20 0.20 0.30 0.30
[12] 0.30 0.47 0.47 0.47 0.47 0.47 0.50 0.64 0.64 0.64 0.73
[23] 0.73 0.82 0.82 1.00 1.00 1.00 1.00 1.00
```

If the thresholds are not themselves empirical cases, the values of the cases closest to but greater than τ_{ex}, and those smaller than τ_{cr} and τ_{in} will be used.

4.2 Testing for Necessity

In this and the following sections, the results from a study on job security regulations in Western democracies by Emmenegger (2011) are replicated. The conditions are a high level of statism (**S**), a high level of non-market coordination (**C**), a high level of labor movement strength (**L**), a high level of Catholicism (**R**), a high level of religious party strength (**P**), and many institutional veto points (**V**). The dataset is integrated in the **QCA** package and can be loaded with the data() function.[11]

```
> data(Emme)
```

As Emmenegger hypothesizes the negation of **V** to be necessary for **JSR**, the set of "countries with not many political veto points" has to be constructed first. We use the fact that for every general set **SET**, set = 1 − **SET**. Emmenegger (2011, p. 347) further argues that a high level of job security regulations can only be expected for high levels of statism (**S**), high levels of non-market coordination (**C**), and high levels of statism or high levels of non-market coordination (**S** + **C**).[12]

```
> Emme$v <- 1 - Emme$V
> Emme$"S+C" <- pmax(Emme$S, Emme$C)
> Emme

      S    C    L    R    P    V   JSR     v   S+C
AU 0.00 0.00 0.57 0.2 0.0 1.00 0.14 0.00 0.00
AT 0.67 1.00 0.57 1.0 0.8 0.67 0.71 0.33 1.00
BE 1.00 0.67 0.43 1.0 1.0 0.67 0.57 0.33 1.00
.. .... .... .... ... ... .... .... .... ....
<<rest omitted>>
```

---

[11] After having loaded the dataset, further information on it can be obtained with the usual help call ?Emme.

[12] Notice that **S** and **C** are both subsets of **S** + **C**. When **S** and/or **C** are/is individually necessary, the combination **S** + **C** must also be necessary.

The set **v** is created by subtracting **V** from 1, and the set **S** + **C** is created using the
pmax() function introduced in Sect. 2.10. Recall that it returns the parallel maxima
of its arguments. Due to the "plus" sign + parentheses have to enclose the set name.

Emmenegger has created these sets in order to test their necessity relations to
the outcome. However, as will be shown later on, QCA does not require users to
manually test for necessity. Conditions can, of course, always be created by the user.
The above was an example of how to achieve this. For our purposes, however, sets
v and **S** + **C** are not needed. They can be dropped by preceding their column index
with a minus operator.

```
> Emme <- Emme[ , -(8:9)]
```

The dataset Emme should now equal the original one again.

4.2.1 Parameters of Fit

Analyses of necessity proceed from the observation of the outcome **O** to the observation of the condition(s) **C**. For analyzing necessity inclusion, the decisive question
is to which degree cases are members of **C** and **O** in relation to their overall membership in **O**. For analyzing necessity coverage, the decisive question is to which
degree cases are members of **C** and **O** in relation to their overall membership in **C**.
If necessity inclusion is high enough, the evidence is consistent with the hypothesis
that **C** is necessary for **O** (**C** ← **O**). If necessity coverage within such a relation is
high enough, the evidence is consistent with the hypothesis that **C** is not trivially
necessary for **O**. The necessity inclusion of **C**, $\text{Incl}_N(\mathbf{C})$, is calculated as given in
Eq. (4.8).

$$\text{Incl}_N(\mathbf{C}) = \frac{\sum_{i=1}^{n} \min(c_i, o_i)}{\sum_{i=1}^{n} o_i} \tag{4.8}$$

The necessity coverage of **C**, $\text{Cov}_N(\mathbf{C})$, is calculated as given in Eq. (4.9).

$$\text{Cov}_N(\mathbf{C}) = \frac{\sum_{i=1}^{n} \min(c_i, o_i)}{\sum_{i=1}^{n} o_i} \tag{4.9}$$

Unlike in csQCA, the use of fuzzy sets in fsQCA sometimes leads to seemingly
paradoxical situations. At worst, the evidence for the existence of a necessity relation
between a condition and the outcome may be as sufficiently strong as the evidence
for the existence of a necessity relation between the negation of this condition and
the outcome. While necessity coverage may or may not remain the same, such a
situation occurs when (almost) all cases fall into area A_1 in Fig. 4.3.

A measure that helps identify such situations is the PRI score (proportional
reduction in inconsistency). While fs/QCA computes the PRI for the sufficiency
relation of each truth table configuration to the outcome set, it does not provide it

Fig. 4.3 "Paradoxical" relations with fuzzy sets

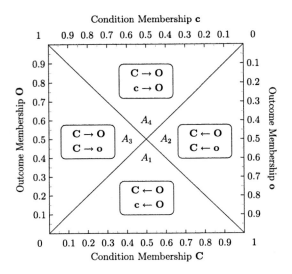

for the analysis of necessity relations. In QCA, the necessity PRI of C, $\mathrm{PRI}_N(C)$, is calculated as given in Eq. (4.10).[13]

$$\mathrm{PRI}_N(C) = \frac{\sum_{i=1}^{n} \min(c_i, o_i) - \sum_{i=1}^{n} \min(c_i, 1 - c_i, o_i)}{\sum_{i=1}^{n} o_i - \sum_{i=1}^{n} \min(c_i, 1 - c_i, o_i)} \qquad (4.10)$$

Necessity PRI ranges from 0 to 1, but it is undefined if all cases fall into area A_1. Then, $\mathrm{Incl}_N(C) = \mathrm{Incl}_N(c)$ because each case's membership in O will always be less than both its membership in C and c. High PRI scores may point towards relatively large differences between $\mathrm{Incl}_N(C)$ and $\mathrm{Incl}_N(c)$, but this is not always true. It depends on the distribution of membership scores in the condition and the outcome. Thus, we caution readers right away against substituting PRI, or its product with the corresponding inclusion score as advocated by fs/QCA and some authors (Schneider and Wagemann, 2012), for a thorough comparison of inclusion scores. QCA comes with suitable functionality to perform extensive testing in this respect as will be shown in the following sections.

4.2.2 Analyzing Necessity Relations

In order to test for necessary conditions, QCA provides the superSubset() function. For the details of its algorithm, see Sect. 3.2.2. In summary, superSubset() does not require a preselection of the combinations to be tested, and so removes the

---

[13] By default, the QCA package also computes PRI scores for binary and multi-value crisp-set data, but in csQCA and mvQCA, PRI always equals inclusion.

risk of leaving potentially interesting results undiscovered. It does not require a specification of the conditions if they represent all other sets but the outcome in the data. The argument `incl.cut` sets the inclusion cut-off and `cov.cut` the coverage cut-off. The algorithm will search as long as it takes to meet these criteria, but if no combination can be found, a warning message will be returned.

Full syntax:

```
> superSubset(Emme, outcome = "JSR", neg.out = FALSE,
+   conditions = names(Emme)[1:6], relation = "necessity",
+   incl.cut = 0.965, cov.cut = 0.6, use.tilde = FALSE,
+   use.letters = FALSE)
```

```
> EmmeNR <- superSubset(Emme, outcome = "JSR",
+   incl.cut = 0.965, cov.cut = 0.6)
> EmmeNR
```

		incl	PRI	cov.r
1	C+R	0.968	0.964	0.722
2	S+C	0.968	0.963	0.691
3	R+P+v	0.975	0.972	0.622
4	L+R+P	0.994	0.993	0.685
5	S+L+P	1.000	1.000	0.669
6	C+L+P+v	0.967	0.963	0.609

No uniliteral combination has met the criteria, but six disjunctive combinations have been found. Two biliteral, three triliteral, and one quadriliteral combination have passed the relatively stringent inclusion and coverage cut-offs. The results from this replication illustrate the advantage of QCA's `superSubset()` function over the user-driven procedures of fs/QCA, QCA3 and fuzzy. Recall that Emmenegger hypothesized the combination $S + C$ to be necessary for **JSR**, but this condition displays the same evidence for the existence of a necessity relation with regard to the outcome as $C + R$. What is more, $Cov_N(C + R) = 0.72$ is larger than $Cov_N(S + C) = 0.69$. We do not judge whether this finding is consistent with theoretical expectations about the relation between **C**, **R** and **JSR**, but only conclude that the union of these two sets performs better than $S + C$.

Figure 4.3 has illustrated why seemingly paradoxical relations can appear in fsQCA. With regard to the analysis of necessity relations, $PRI_N(C)$ has been introduced in order to account for the fact that cases in area A_1 confirm a situation in which **C** as well as **c** can be considered necessary for **O**.

In addition to returning combinations of conditions and their parameters of fit, the `superSubset()` function also generates an invisible component called `coms`.

This component contains each case's <u>c</u>ombination <u>m</u>embership <u>s</u>cores. As coms is a data frame, all columns can be accessed as shown in Sect. 2.8. The combinations of membership scores for the first three cases are shown below.

```
> EmmeNR$coms[1:3, ]

   C+R S+C R+P+v L+R+P S+L+P C+L+P+v
AU 0.2   0   0.2  0.57  0.57    0.57
AT 1.0   1   1.0  1.00  0.80    1.00
BE 1.0   1   1.0  1.00  1.00    1.00
```

The coms component can then be passed directly to QCA's pof() function, which is a generic and flexible function for computing inclusion, PRI, and coverage scores for both necessity and sufficiency relations. At a minimum, it requires a data frame of set membership scores, the original dataset and the identification of the outcome set. In order to analyze necessity inclusion for the negation of all combinations found by superSubset() and saved in EmmeNR, the coms component just has to be negated.

Full syntax:

```
> pof(1 - EmmeNR$coms, Emme, outcome = "JSR", neg.out = FALSE,
+   relation = "necessity")
```

```
> pof(1 - EmmeNR$coms, Emme, outcome = "JSR")

              incl   PRI    cov.r
-------------------------------------
1   C+R       0.147  0.032  0.263
2   S+C       0.162  0.032  0.325
3   R+P+v     0.101  0.000  0.303
4   L+R+P     0.139  0.000  0.310
5   S+L+P     0.154  0.000  0.380
6   C+L+P+v   0.110  0.000  0.354
-------------------------------------
```

These results confirm that, overall, only few cases fall into area A_1. All necessity inclusion scores of the negated combinations are far too low to indicate a possible necessity relation to JSR. On the other hand, this may come at the cost of the original combinations being only trivially necessary. As the coverage cut-off had already been set to 0.6 in superSubset(), but did not exceed 0.73 for any combination, coverage can still be considered moderately high.

A second problematic area in the analysis of necessity relations is A_2 in Fig. 4.3. Here, the evidence for the existence of a necessity relation between a condition and the outcome may be as sufficiently strong as the evidence for the existence of a necessity relation between the condition and the negation of the outcome. Whether this is the case can also be tested with the pof() function. Its argument neg.out controls the outcome set.

```
> pof(EmmeNR$coms, Emme, outcome = "JSR", neg.out = TRUE)
```

		incl	PRI	cov.r
1	C+R	0.542	0.461	0.364
2	S+C	0.626	0.544	0.402
3	R+P+v	0.742	0.714	0.426
4	L+R+P	0.657	0.560	0.407
5	S+L+P	0.721	0.635	0.434
6	C+L+P+v	0.777	0.747	0.440

No inclusion score is sufficiently high to indicate that a combination may be necessary for the outcome as well as its negation.

4.2.3 Plotting Results

The relationship $S + C \leftarrow JSR$ is plotted in Fig. 4.1, (Emmenegger 2011, p. 347). This plot is reproduced in Fig. 4.4 below. First, the basic plot is generated with the plot() function. The abscissa values are given by the set membership scores for condition $S + C$ and the ordinate values by the set membership scores for the outcome JSR. The optional arguments pch, ylab and xlab define the marker symbol (a black dot) and the respective axis label.

```
> plot(EmmeNR$coms$"S+C", Emme$JSR, pch = 19,
+  xlab = "S + C", ylab = "JSR")
```

With the plotting device opened, the diagonal line representing set identity can be added with the abline() function.

```
> abline(0, 1)
```

The first argument in abline() is the intercept, the slope the second. To complete the plot, all that remains is to identify the cases that are of further analytical importance.[14] Keep the plotting device open and enter the following code:

```
> cases <- c(1, 3, 11, 14, 17)
> text(EmmeNR$coms$"S+C"[cases], Emme$JSR[cases],
+  labels = rownames(Emme)[cases],
+  pos = c(4, rep(2, 4)))
```

---

[14] Labeling all cases, as in Fig. 1, Emmenegger (2011, p. 347) is usually not necessary.

Fig. 4.4 Necessity relation
between **S + C** and **JSR**

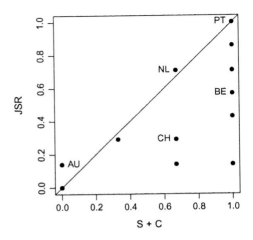

First, we create the vector of row numbers `cases` which identifies all important
cases. With the help of the `text()` function, case labels can be added. The first
argument is again the vector of abscissa values, the second the vector of ordinate values. Instead of manually creating a character vector of case labels, the `rownames()`
function has been used for the `labels` argument. The `pos` argument then positions
all labels around the case markers.[15]

With the plotting device window open, cases can also easily be labeled interac-
tively with the `identify()` function (not shown here).[16]

```
> identify(EmmeNR$coms$"S+C", Emme$JSR, labels = rownames(Emme),
+  plot = TRUE)
```

The first two arguments specify all possible coordinates and the `labels` argument
the vector of case labels which correspond to these coordinates. The last argument
`plot = TRUE` simply causes the labels to be printed near the case markers.[17]

4.3 Testing for Sufficiency

The ultimate goal of QCA is to analyze set-theoretic sufficiency relations (Ragin
2009, p. 110), for which the construction of the truth table is central. In addition to the
exhaustive formation of all configurations, an outcome value for each configuration
has to be established. An outcome value represents a fractional truth value of the

---

[15] 1, 2, 3, and 4 stand for below, to the left, above, and to the right.

[16] As the `identify()` function will only label each pair of coordinates once, check whether some
cases have exactly the same values and overlap each other on a single point, for example with a
cross-tabulation of fuzzy-set membership scores.

[17] For more options such as label offsets and identification tolerance, enter `?identify`.

statement that aggregate case membership in the corresponding corner of the 2^k-cornered vector space is equal to or lower than aggregate case membership in the outcome set.

4.3.1 Parameters of Fit

Analyses of sufficiency proceed from the observation of some condition(s) **C** to the observation of the outcome **O**. For analyzing sufficiency inclusion, the decisive question is to which degree cases are members of **C** and **O** in relation to their overall membership in **C**. For analyzing sufficiency coverage, the decisive question is to which degree cases are members of **C** and **O** in relation to their overall membership in **O**. If sufficiency inclusion is high enough, the evidence is consistent with the hypothesis that **C** is sufficient for **O** (**C** → **O**). If sufficiency coverage within such a relation is high enough, the evidence is consistent with the hypothesis that **C** is not trivially sufficient for **O**. The sufficiency inclusion of **C**, $\mathrm{Incl}_S(\mathbf{C})$, is calculated as given in Eq. (4.11).

$$\mathrm{Incl}_S(\mathbf{C}) = \frac{\sum_{i=1}^{n} \min(c_i, o_i)}{\sum_{i=1}^{n} c_i}. \tag{4.11}$$

The sufficiency coverage of **C**, $\mathrm{Cov}_S(\mathbf{C})$, is calculated as given in Eq. (4.12).

$$\mathrm{Cov}_S(\mathbf{C}) = \frac{\sum_{i=1}^{n} \min(c_i, o_i)}{\sum_{i=1}^{n} o_i}. \tag{4.12}$$

Three different types of sufficiency coverage exist. Raw coverage can refer to a minimal sum or a PI within a minimal sum. Unique coverage refers to that part of each PI's raw coverage which is not shared by any other PI within the same minimal sum.

As in the case of analyzing necessity relations, the use of fuzzy sets sometimes leads to seemingly paradoxical situations in which the evidence for the existence of a sufficiency relation between a condition and the outcome may be as sufficiently strong as the evidence for the existence of a sufficiency relation between this condition and the negation of the outcome (Cooper and Glaesser 2011). While sufficiency coverage may or may not remain the same, such a situation occurs when (almost) all cases fall into area A_3 in Fig. 4.3. The **fs/QCA** software, for example, computes the PRI for each configuration in the truth table. PRI for sufficiency relations $\mathrm{PRI}_S(\mathbf{C})$ is calculated as given in Eq. (4.13).

$$\mathrm{PRI}_S(\mathbf{C}) = \frac{\sum_{i=1}^{n} \min(c_i, o_i) - \sum_{i=1}^{n} \min(c_i, o_i, 1 - o_i)}{\sum_{i=1}^{n} c_i - \sum_{i=1}^{n} \min(c_i, o_i, 1 - o_i)} \tag{4.13}$$

Sufficiency PRI ranges from 0 to 1, but it is undefined if all cases fall into area A_3. Then, $\mathrm{Incl}_S(\mathbf{C} \rightarrow \mathbf{O}) = \mathrm{Incl}_S(\mathbf{C} \rightarrow \mathbf{o})$ because each case's membership in $\mathbf{C}$ will always be less than both its membership in $\mathbf{O}$ and $\mathbf{o}$. High PRI scores may point towards relatively large differences between $\mathrm{Incl}_S(\mathbf{C} \rightarrow \mathbf{O})$ and $\mathrm{Incl}_S(\mathbf{C} \rightarrow \mathbf{o})$, but this is not always true. It depends on the distribution of membership scores in the condition and the outcome. To reiterate the point made in Sect. 4.2.1, PRI should not substitute for a thorough comparison of inclusion scores.

4.3.2 Constructing the Truth Table

Just as for crisp-set data, the truthTable() function also constructs truth tables from fuzzy-set data. At the very least, it requires two arguments: a matrix or data frame of fuzzy-set membership scores and an outcome set. In order to create the truth table object EmmeTT, the dataset Emme is specified as the first argument, then the outcome set **JSR**. If not all columns except the one representing the outcome set are to be selected as conditions, the conditions argument must also be specified. As all sets but **JSR** are conditions, the eponymous argument need not be provided.

```
Full syntax:

> EmmeTT <- truthTable(Emme, outcome = "JSR", neg.out = FALSE,
+   conditions = names(Emme)[1:6], n.cut = 1, incl.cut1 = 0.9,
+   incl.cut0 = 0.9, complete = FALSE, show.cases = TRUE,
+   sort.by = c("incl", "n"), decreasing = TRUE,
+   use.letters = FALSE)
```

```
> EmmeTT <- truthTable(Emme, outcome = "JSR", incl.cut1 = 0.9,
+   show.cases = TRUE, sort.by = c("incl", "n"))
> EmmeTT

 OUT: outcome value
   n: number of cases in configuration
incl: sufficiency inclusion score
 PRI: proportional reduction in inconsistency
```

	S	C	L	R	P	V	OUT	n	incl	PRI	cases
56	1	1	0	1	1	1	1	2	1.000	1.000	BE,DE
47	1	0	1	1	1	0	1	1	1.000	1.000	IT
48	1	0	1	1	1	1	1	1	1.000	1.000	ES
64	1	1	1	1	1	1	1	1	1.000	1.000	AT
37	1	0	0	1	0	0	1	2	0.977	0.966	FR,PT
27	0	1	1	0	1	0	1	1	0.940	0.825	NO

```
25  0  1  1  0  0  0    0  2  0.839 0.699 DK,SE
57  1  1  1  0  0  0    0  1  0.717 0.000 FI
20  0  1  0  0  1  1    0  2  0.716 0.500 NL,CH
 5  0  0  0  1  0  0    0  1  0.581 0.000 IE
10  0  0  1  0  0  1    0  1  0.494 0.000 AU
33  1  0  0  0  0  0    0  2  0.203 0.000 NZ,GB
 2  0  0  0  0  0  1    0  2  0.198 0.000 CA,US
```

The `truthTable()` function includes three cut-off arguments that influence how a configuration is coded in the outcome value column "OUT": `n.cut`, `incl.cut1` and `incl.cut0`. The first argument `n.cut` specifies the minimum number of cases with membership above 0.5 needed in order to not code a configuration as a logical remainder as indicated by "?". The second argument `incl.cut1` specifies the minimal sufficiency inclusion score for a non-remainder configuration to be coded as true ("1"). The third argument `incl.cut0` offers the possibility of coding configurations as contradictions ("C") when their inclusion score is neither high nor low enough to consider them as true, respectively false. If the inclusion score of a non-remainder configuration falls below `incl.cut0`, it is always coded false ("0").

By default, `truthTable()` only returns those configurations of the truth table in which at least `n.cut` cases have membership above 0.5. The names of these cases are printed if the `show.cases` argument is set to TRUE. With the `sort.by` argument, the truth table can also be ordered along inclusion scores, numbers of cases, or both. The logical argument `decreasing` controls the sorting order.

4.3.3 Boolean Minimization

The minimization of the canonical sum whose fundamental products correspond to all true configurations yields the *complex solution*. The derivation of this solution type is achieved with the `eqmcc()` function (enhanced Quine-McCluskey) (Duşa 2007a, 2010). This is the core function of the **QCA** package.

Full syntax:

```
> EmmeSC <- eqmcc(EmmeTT, explain = "1", include = "1",
+   all.sol = FALSE, omit = c(), direxp = c(), rowdom = TRUE,
+   details = TRUE, show.cases = TRUE, use.tilde = FALSE,
+   use.letters = FALSE)
```

```
> EmmeSC <- eqmcc(EmmeTT, details = TRUE, show.cases = TRUE)
```

The truth table object EmmeTT is passed to eqmcc() as the first argument.[18] By default, true configurations are explained. No additional information is required for arriving at the complex solution. The all.sol argument causes eqmcc() to derive all minimal sums of the solution, not just those with the fewest PIs.[19] The logical argument details causes all parameters of fit to be printed together with the minimal sum: inclusion, PRI, raw coverage, and unique coverage scores for each PI as well as the minimal sum.[20] The logical argument show.cases also prints the names of the cases that are covered by each PI if details = TRUE.

```
> EmmeSC

n OUT = 1/0/C: 8/11/0
  Total      : 19


Number of multiple-covered cases: 0

S1: ScLRP + SCRPV + sCLrPv + SclRpv


            incl   PRI    cov.r  cov.u  cases
    ------------------------------------------------
1   ScLRP   1.000  1.000  0.204  0.055  IT; ES
2   SCRPV   0.960  0.921  0.237  0.151  BE,DE;  AT
3   sCLrPv  0.940  0.825  0.171  0.171  NO
4   SclRpv  0.977  0.966  0.172  0.089  FR,PT
    ------------------------------------------------
    S1      0.961  0.931  0.615
```

The output which is printed when an object returned by eqmcc() is called up consists of three parts. The header provides information about the number of cases in each of the three types of configurations in which cases have membership above 0.5, and the total number of cases. If show.cases = TRUE, it also displays the number of cases which are covered by more than one PI. The middle part prints the solution, which may consist of one or more minimal sums S. The bottom part provides the parameters-of-fit (POF) table.

The minimal sum consists of four PIs. These terms cover eight cases across six configurations, namely Spain and Italy in the first term, Norway in the second, France and Portugal in the third, and Austria, Belgium and Germany in the fourth term. No case is covered by more than one PI. Cases from the same configuration are separated by a comma, those from different configurations by a semicolon.

---

[18] The eqmcc() function can also directly process datasets with fuzzy-set membership scores. However, it is recommended that the function only be used after having created and evaluated the truth table.

[19] This argument has been suggested by Michael Baumgartner.

[20] Unique coverage scores do not apply to minimal sums.

Sometimes it is desired that common literals across different PIs be emphasized in solutions. For this purpose, minimal sums can be factorized using QCA's `factorize()` function.

```
> factorize(EmmeSC)

S: ScLRP + SCRPV + sCLrPv + SclRpv

F1: v(sCLrP + SclRp) + PRS(cL + CV)
F2: RS(cLP + CPV + clpv) + sCLrPv
F3: CP(SRV + sLrv) + cRS(LP + lpv)
F4: LP(ScR + sCrv) + RS(CPV + clpv)
F5: P(ScLR + SCRV + sCLrv) + SclRpv
```

There exist five possibilities for factorizing the complex solution. The one which best underlines the theoretical argument to be made in the analysis should ideally be chosen. If the importance of **P** is to be stressed, F_5 provides a suitable representation.

4.3.4 Incorporating Logical Remainders

Logical remainders are configurations for which no case possesses a membership score above 0.5, or which have been judged to contain too few cases in relation to the total number of cases. However, each single such configuration provides a potentially relevant combination of conditions that allows researchers to engage in counterfactual thinking. Two common solution types which rely on counterfactuals are the parsimonious and the intermediate solution. Before logical remainders can be incorporated into the analysis, a new object which contains the entire truth table should be created. The provision of the additional argument `complete = TRUE` in the `truthTable()` function generates the entire truth table. For reasons of space, it is not called up here.

```
> EmmeTT <- truthTable(Emme, outcome = "JSR",
+    incl.cut1 = 0.9, complete = TRUE)
```

With `EmmeTT` now containing the complete truth table, it becomes possible to generate solution types which incorporate logical remainders.

4.3.4.1 Parsimonious Solution

If all logical remainders are made available for minimization, the minimal sum(s) obtained from this process are summarized under the *parsimonious solution*. Logical remainders can be incorporated into the minimization process by using the `include` argument in `eqmcc()`. Ignore the `rowdom` argument for the moment.

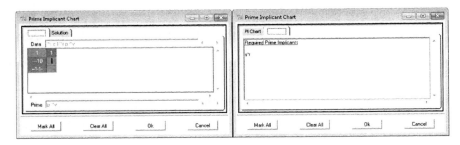

Fig. 4.5 PI Chart Window (*Emmenegger*) in fs/QCA

```
> EmmeSP <- eqmcc(EmmeTT, include = "?", rowdom = FALSE,
+   details = TRUE)
> EmmeSP

n OUT = 1/0/C: 8/11/0
  Total      : 19

S1: SR + (LP)
S2: SR + (Pv)

                         -------------------
         incl   PRI    cov.r  cov.u  (S1)    (S2)
       ---------------------------------------------
 1  SR  0.871  0.821  0.610  0.231  0.256   0.335
       ---------------------------------------------
 2  LP  0.979  0.955  0.506  0.014  0.152
 3  Pv  0.950  0.883  0.417  0.004          0.142
       ---------------------------------------------
     S1  0.883  0.821  0.762
     S2  0.874  0.812  0.752
```

The parsimonious solution consists of the two minimal sums S_1 and S_2, each of which contains two PIs. This situation is the analogy of choosing all inessential PIs in the PI chart of fs/QCA with the *Mark All* button in the bottom-left part of the window. It is shown in Fig. 4.5. The *Data* line in this window indicates that the fundamental product $s \cdot C \cdot L \cdot r \cdot P \cdot v$ is covered by *Prime* $P \cdot v$ as well as $L \cdot P$. These two PIs are not listed in the *Solution* tab, which shows all essential PIs, but at least one is required to complete a minimal sum, so users are asked to choose one of the inessential PIs or both.

In QCA's solution output, inessential PIs are enclosed by brackets and listed in the middle part of the POF table below the solution, while essential PIs are listed in the upper part. The bottom part shows all parameters of fit for each minimal sum. If there are multiple minimal sums, unique coverage may vary, for both essential and inessential PIs. The columns with the respective headers for each minimal sum are therefore listed next to the unique coverage column cov.u.

Although there is nothing wrong in choosing both inessential PIs, $\mathbf{L} \cdot \mathbf{P}$ in fact dominates $\mathbf{P} \cdot \mathbf{v}$. One PI P_1 is said to dominate another P_2 if all fundamental products covered by P_2 are also covered by P_1 and both are not interchangeable. This principle is often referred to as *row dominance* because in PI charts, columns represent fundamental products and rows the PIs. The application of the row dominance principle is controlled through the rowdom argument in eqmcc(). When set to its default value TRUE, the dominated inessential PI is always eliminated from the solution. When set to FALSE, dominated PIs are retained.[21]

That $\mathbf{L} \cdot \mathbf{P}$ really dominates $\mathbf{P} \cdot \mathbf{v}$ in the parsimonious solution can be seen when calling up the subcomponent p.sol in the PI chart component PIchart of the QCA solution object created by eqmcc().

```
> EmmeSP$PIchart$p.sol

     27 37 47 48 56 64
..    .  .  .  .  .  .
LP    x  -  x  x  -  x
..    .  .  .  .  .  .
Pv    x  -  x  -  -  -
..    .  .  .  .  .  .
SR    -  x  x  x  x  x
..    .  .  .  .  .  .
```

Truth table rows 27 and 47 are implied by $\mathbf{P} \cdot \mathbf{v}$, but so are they by $\mathbf{L} \cdot \mathbf{P}$. Both PIs are not interchangeable because $\mathbf{L} \cdot \mathbf{P}$ also implies truth table rows 48 and 64 in addition. As row 47 is also implied by $\mathbf{S} \cdot \mathbf{R}$, row 27 must correspond to the fundamental product for which $\mathbf{P} \cdot \mathbf{v}$ and $\mathbf{L} \cdot \mathbf{P}$ are alternatives. Using this row name, the configuration in question can be found by accessing the tt component of the truth table object. We also index the columns because only the raw configuration is of interest.[22]

```
> EmmeTT$tt["27", 1:6]

    S C L R P V
27  0 1 1 0 1 0
```

In this regard, the simplifying assumptions (SA) on which the derivation of the parsimonious solution has been based may also be of interest. The SAs of S_2 can be called up by accessing its subcomponent in the overall list component SA returned by eqmcc().

---

[21] It may happen that there are multiple inessential PIs, none of which dominates the other.

[22] It is important to use double quotes around the number 27 because row names are of data type *character*. Alternatively, truth table rows can also be accessed in the solution object. The same output would have been generated by EmmeSPtttt["27", 1:6].

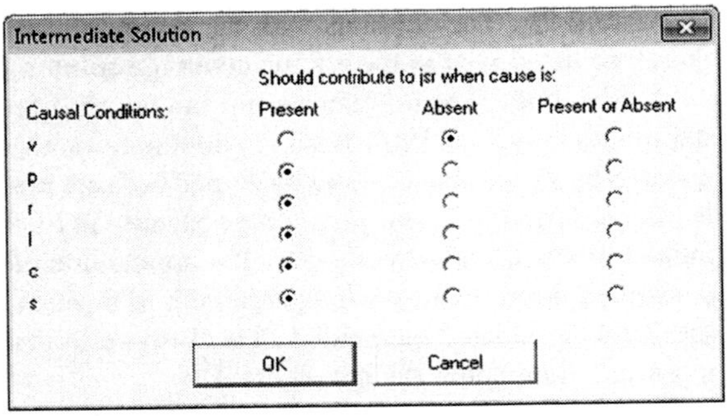

Fig. 4.6 Directional expectations window in fs/QCA

> *EmmeSPSAS1*

```
   S C L R P V
11 0 0 1 0 1 0
12 0 0 1 0 1 1
15 0 0 1 1 1 0
. . . . . . .
<<rest omitted>>
```

Twenty-two logical remainders have been used as SAs in the derivation of S_1.

4.3.4.2 Intermediate Solution

If researchers make explicit assumptions about the set-theoretic relationship between
a condition and the outcome by formulating *directional expectations*, the result is
called the *intermediate solution*. The intermediate solution is always a subset of
the parsimonious solution, so it does not use any logical remainders as simplifying
assumptions other than those which have already been used in the derivation of
the parsimonious solution. The complex and the parsimonious solution are always
unique, but the intermediate solution is not. Essentially, it consists of the entire set of
possible solutions between the complex and the parsimonious solution. In fs/QCA,
the window where directional expectations are specified is shown in Fig. 4.5. Radio
buttons, shown in Fig. 4.6, specify whether there is an expectation, and if so, which
direction it has.

Intermediate solutions can be generated in QCA by making use of the direxp
argument. This takes a numeric vector whose length and order equals the number
and arrangement of conditions in the truth table. The value "1" indicates that the
condition is expected to contribute to an outcome value of "1," "0" that it is the
negation of this condition. The value "-1" indicates that no directional expectations
are made. Conditions **C, L, P, R** and **S** are all expected to contribute to OUT = 1
when present, whereas **V** is expected to do so when absent.

```
> EmmeSI <- eqmcc(EmmeTT, include = "?",
+  direxp = c(1,1,1,1,1,0), details = TRUE, show.cases = TRUE)
> EmmeSI
```

```
n OUT = 1/0/C: 8/11/0
  Total       : 19
```

```
p.sol: LP + SR
```

```
Number of multiple-covered cases: 2
```

```
S1:    SRv + CLPv + SCRP + SLRP
```

		incl	PRI	cov.r	cov.u	cases
1	SRv	0.990	0.983	0.402	0.152	FR,PT; IT
2	CLPv	0.964	0.872	0.297	0.138	NO
3	SCRP	0.965	0.921	0.277	0.041	BE,DE; AT
4	SLRP	1.000	1.000	0.354	0.027	IT; ES; AT
	S1	0.965	0.941	0.685		

The printed output for intermediate solutions contains an additional line between the header and the solution part for that minimal sum of the parsimonious solution p.sol from which the intermediate solution has been derived. This implies that if rowdom had been set to FALSE, there would have been two intermediate solutions.

4.3.4.3 Contradictory Simplifying Assumptions

Contradictory simplifying assumptions (CSA) are logical remainders which enter into the derivation of the solution with respect to the outcome set as well as its negation. Reconsider the first minimal sum of the parsimonious solution, S_1: $S \cdot R + L \cdot P$. First, the minimization has to be carried out for the negation of the outcome. As neither the truth table nor the solution details are of immediate interest here, the eqmcc() function can be called directly on the original dataset instead of the truth table. If the object passed to eqmcc() is not a truth table object but a data frame or matrix of set data, the logical argument neg.out negates the outcome.[23]

```
> EmmeSPn <- eqmcc(Emme, outcome = "JSR", neg.out = TRUE,
+  incl.cut1 = 0.9, include = "?")
> EmmeSPn
```

```
S1: sc + Sr
```

---

[23] If a truth table object is passed to eqmcc(), the neg.out argument has no effect.

The parsimonious solution for the negation of the outcome set consists of one minimal sum. How to access SAs has been shown above in Sect. 4.3.4.1. First, a vectors of those truth table row names is generated which identifies the respective SAs for the minimal sum. They can be extracted with the `rownames()` function.

```
> (SAs1n <- rownames(EmmeSPn$SA$S1))

 [1]  "1"   "3"   "4"   "6"   "7"   "8"   "9"   "11"  "12"  "13"  "14"
[12]  "15"  "16"  "34"  "35"  "36"  "41"  "42"  "43"  "44"  "49"  "50"
[23]  "51"  "52"  "58"  "59"  "60"
```

Second, we need the SAs for minimal sum S_1 from the original analysis performed in Sect. 4.3.4.1.

```
> (SAs1 <- rownames(EmmeSP$SA$S1))

 [1]  "11"  "12"  "15"  "16"  "28"  "31"  "32"  "38"  "39"  "40"  "43"
[12]  "44"  "45"  "46"  "53"  "54"  "55"  "59"  "60"  "61"  "62"  "63"
```

With only relatively few SAs, visual inspection may be sufficient. However, it is always better to apply a formal test, in particular when the numbers of SAs become larger. Most suitably, the `intersect()` function introduced in Sect. 2.9 can be employed to test whether there exist any shared SAs.

```
> (CSA <- intersect(SAs1n, SAs1))

[1]  "11"  "12"  "15"  "16"  "43"  "44"  "59"  "60"
```

Contradictory assumptions are made on eight logical remainders. By using the character vector CSA to index the truth table component of EmmeTT, the exact configurations can be found.

```
> EmmeTT$tt[CSA, ]
```

	S	C	L	R	P	V	OUT	n	incl	PRI
11	0	0	1	0	1	0	?	0	0.935483870967742	0
12	0	0	1	0	1	1	?	0	1	–
15	0	0	1	1	1	0	?	0	0.940298507462687	0
16	0	0	1	1	1	1	?	0	1	–
43	1	0	1	0	1	0	?	0	–	–
44	1	0	1	0	1	1	?	0	–	–
59	1	1	1	0	1	0	?	0	1	–
60	1	1	1	0	1	1	?	0	1	1

4.3.5 Further Diagnostics

Figure 4.3 has illustrated why seemingly paradoxical relations can appear in fsQCA. With regard to the analysis of sufficiency relations, $PRI_S(C)$ has been introduced in order to account for the fact that cases in area A_3 confirm a situation in which **C** can be considered sufficient for **O** as well as **o**.

Similar to the coms component in objects returned by superSubset(), eqmcc() returns a pims component, which contains all PI membership scores. The relevant subcomponent of pims for the intermediate solution is i.sol. The last piece of information that is needed concerns the respective complex and parsimonious solution from which the intermediate solution has been formed. The row dominance principle has been applied in the derivation of EmmeSI, and we know that the parsimonious solution only contains one minimal sum. As intermediate solutions always result from a unique combination of a minimal sum from the complex solution and one from the parsimonious solution, the identifier in the solution subcomponent of pims indexes the respective combination. In our example, the combination of the first (and only) minimal sum $S1$ from the complex solution and the first (and only) minimal sum $S1$ from the parsimonious solution is indexed by C1P1.

```
> pof(EmmeSI$pims$i.sol$C1P1, Emme, outcome = "JSR",
+   neg.out = TRUE, relation = "sufficiency")

          incl    PRI    cov.r   cov.u
----------------------------------------
1  SRv    0.438   0.017  0.198   0.031
2  CLPv   0.756   0.128  0.259   0.108
3  SCRP   0.557   0.000  0.178   0.000
4  SLRP   0.492   0.000  0.193   0.000
----------------------------------------
```

None of the PIs shows a high enough inclusion score in relation to the negated outcome **jsr**. Only **C · L · P · v** has an inclusion score above 0.75, but this is still significantly lower than that for the original outcome set **JSR**.

A second area that is problematic for the analysis of sufficiency relations is A_4 in Fig. 4.3. Here, the evidence for the existence of a sufficiency relation between a condition and the outcome may be as strong as the evidence for the existence of a sufficiency relation between the negation of the condition and the outcome. Whether this is the case can also be tested with the pof() function by negating all PIs.

```
> pof(1 - EmmeSI$pims$i.sol$C1P1, Emme, outcome = "JSR",
+   relation = "sufficiency")

         incl   PRI    cov.r  cov.u
  ----------------------------------------
1  SRv    0.517  0.357  0.772  0.000
2  CLPv   0.581  0.453  0.925  0.000
3  SCRP   0.541  0.408  0.873  0.000
4  SLRP   0.530  0.382  0.820  0.000
  ----------------------------------------
```

Just as for the negation of the outcome, the inclusion score of no negated PI would be considered high enough to confirm sufficiency.

4.3.6 Plotting Results

In order to round off the analysis, the results for all four PIs from the intermediate solution are to be plotted as shown in Fig. 4.7. We first need the membership scores of each case in each PI. To do this, we again exploit the pims component in the object returned by the eqmcc() function as previously shown for the identification of CSAs.

```
> (PIsc <- EmmeSI$pims$i.sol$C1P1)

     SRv  CLPv SCRP SLRP
AU 0.00 0.00 0.00 0.00
AT 0.33 0.33 0.67 0.57
BE 0.33 0.33 0.67 0.43
.. .... .... .... ....
<<rest omitted>>
```

Instead of four single plot() commands, the for(){...} loop construct can be used.[24]

```
> par(mfrow = c(2, 2))
> for(i in 1:4){
+   plot(PIsc[ , i], Emme$JSR, pch = 19, ylab = "JSR",
+   xlab = colnames(PIsc)[i], xlim = c(0, 1), ylim = c(0, 1),
+   main = paste("PI", print(i)))
+   abline(0, 1)
+ }
```

---

[24] Loops are a more advanced programming technique. Alternatively, individual plots can be produced as shown in Sect. 4.2.3.

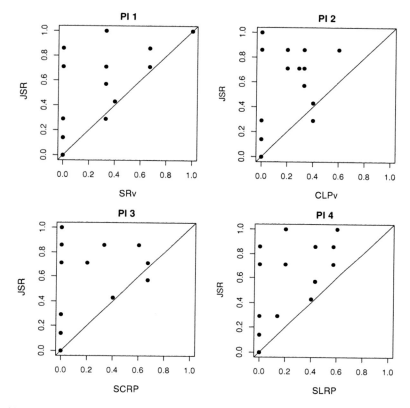

Fig. 4.7 Plots of intermediate solution PIs

First, a plotting device containing four regions is set up with the general graphics parameter function par().[25] The mfrow argument is useful for placing multiple figures into a single row.[26] It takes a numeric vector of length two with the number of rows and the number of figures (columns) to be plotted. Plots are placed one after the other into the separate windows, going by rows. The main title applies the paste() command, putting a fixed text string and the loop counter together. The abline() function adds the straight diagonal line by taking an ordinate intercept and slope parameter as its arguments.[27]

---

[25] See also split.screen() and layout() for similar functionality.

[26] The analogous argument for multiple column figures is mfcol.

[27] If you want to add line segments to a plot, use the segments() function for single lines and the lines() function for joined segments.

Chapter 5
QCA Extensions

Abstract In this chapter, we briefly introduce two extensions of the basic binary-valued crisp-set variant of QCA. The first, multi-value QCA (mvQCA), is essentially a generalization rather than an extension of csQCA. It can accommodate conditions with more than two categories, but remains crisp in that membership in each of these categories cannot be partial and is mutually exclusive. It will also be shown how to plot mvQCA solutions in Venn diagrams and produce intermediate solutions with multi-value data. In contrast, tQCA is a specific kind of csQCA with one or more auxiliary binary-valued crisp conditions whose values denote temporal relations between two or more of the substantive conditions.

5.1 Multi-Value QCA

Multi-value QCA (mvQCA) is a variant of QCA introduced by Lasse Cronqvist, who also developed the **Tosmana** software for performing it (Cronqvist and Berg-Schlosser 2009; Cronqvist 2011). mvQCA is a generalization of csQCA, but it is neither a generalization nor a special case of fsQCA. csQCA can be considered a special case of mvQCA with only two categories, one for denoting the presence of the condition and one for denoting its absence. Furthermore, in csQCA, the number of configurations d_{cs} with k conditions is given by $d_{cs} = 2^k$. In mvQCA the number of configurations d_{mv} with k conditions is given by $d_{mv} = \prod_{j=1}^{k} p_j$, where p_j is the number of values for condition j. However, d_{mv} is the generalization of d_{cs}, the latter being the special case where all $p_j = 2$.

For demonstrating how mvQCA can be performed with **QCA**, we use the study by Hartmann and Kammerzell (2010) on the legal provision and actual implementation of party bans in Sub-Saharan Africa. Its findings with respect to the introduction of party ban provisions (**PB**: 1-yes, 0-no) will be replicated. The conditions are colonial tradition (**C**: 2-British, 1-French, 0-other), former regime type competition

A. Thiem and A. Duşa, *Qualitative Comparative Analysis with R*,
SpringerBriefs in Political Science, DOI: 10.1007/978-1-4614-4584-5_5,
© The Author(s) 2013

(**F**: 2-no, 1-limited, 0-multi-party), the mode of transition (**T**: 2-managed, 1-pacted, 0-democracy before 1990), and ethnic violence (**V**: 1-yes, 0-no).[1]

```
> data(HarKem)
> HarKem

   C F T R V PB PBI
A0 0 2 1 2 1  1   1
BJ 1 2 1 0 0  1   0
BW 2 0 0 0 0  0   0
.. . . . . .  .
<<rest omitted>>
```

As the **QCA** package computes all usual parameters of fit for multi-value data, all functions introduced in relation to csQCA and fsQCA above can be used in exactly the same way. The only difference is the notation. The next sections will therefore not repeat theoretical points or the explanation of computing procedures, except where these relate to particularities of performing mvQCA. Note that the **QCA** package requires multi-value crisp-set categories to start with "0" and increment by 1.

5.1.1 Analyzing Necessity Relations

The **Tosmana** software neither analyzes necessity relations nor does it produce parameters of fit. **QCA** addresses this gap by generalizing the formulas for both inclusion and coverage in csQCA, presented in Sect. 3.2.1, to mvQCA. If $C\{v_l\}$ denotes a general condition level with $l = 1, 2, \ldots, p$, the necessity inclusion of this condition level, $Incl_N(C\{v_l\})$, is then given by Eq. (5.1).

$$Incl_N(C\{v_l\}) = \frac{\sum_{i=1}^{n} \{v_l\}\, c_i = 1|o_i = 1}{\sum_{i=1}^{n} o_i = 1} \qquad (5.1)$$

Equation (5.1) resembles Eq. (3.1) for csQCA, the only difference being that the category of which a case is a member has been added. As categories are mutually exclusive, no ambiguities arise. Accordingly, the necessity coverage of condition level $C\{v_l\}$, $Cov_N(C\{v_l\})$, is then given by Eq. (5.2).

$$Cov_N(C\{v_l\}) = \frac{\sum_{i=1}^{n} \{v_l\}\, c_i = 1|o_i = 1}{\sum_{i=1}^{n} \{v_l\}\, c_i = 1} \qquad (5.2)$$

---

[1] There are four typos in the truth table on page 652, Hartmann and Kammerzell (2010). Botswana, Mauritius, South Africa, and Zimbabwe should be coded as "2" - having a British colonial tradition - not "0". As a result, the solution presented on page 652 is incorrect. The correct solution is given in the Appendix on page 664.

Whether or not any condition level is individually necessary can again be tested with the superSubset() function, which automatically recognizes when at least one condition has a multi-value data structure.

```
> HarKemNR <- superSubset(HarKem, outcome = "PB",
+   conditions = c("C", "F", "T", "V"), incl.cut = 0.9,
+   cov.cut = 0.906)
> HarKemNR
```

```
                      incl   PRI   cov.r
------------------------------------------
1   T{2}+V{0}         0.929 0.929 0.907
2   F{2}+V{0}         0.905 0.905 0.950
3   C{1}+T{2}         0.905 0.905 0.950
4   C{0}+T{1}+V{0}    0.905 0.905 0.927
5   C{0}+F{1}+V{0}    0.929 0.929 0.907
------------------------------------------
```

No single category shows a sufficiently high enough necessity inclusion score, but the three disjunctive combinations of order two $T\{2\} + V\{0\}$, $F\{2\} + V\{0\}$ and $C\{1\} + T\{2\}$ do. As in csQCA, the best way to plot results from an mvQCA is to use Venn diagrams. Although Tosmana has been developed for mvQCA, it is not possible to use its Visualizer tool for multi-value data. However, the VennDiagram package, already introduced and described in more detail for csQCA in Chap. 3, can also be used for visualizing multi-value data in R. The package must first be installed and loaded as shown in Sect. 2.2.

The superSubset() function returns important components that are not directly visible to the end-user in its printed output. One of these invisible yet useful components is coms, which contains all combination membership scores of the combinations found by superSubset(). The coms component is a data frame, all of whose columns can be accessed as usual.

```
> (COms <- HarKemNR$coms[ , 1:3])
```

```
      T{2}+V{0} F{2}+V{0} C{1}+T{2}
A0        0         1         0
BJ        1         1         1
BW        1         1         0
..        .         .         .
<<rest omitted>>
```

With the coms component, users are spared from long Boolean calculations with the pmin() and pmax() functions, and the three combinations can easily be plotted with the venn.diagram() function.[2]

---

[2] The VennDiagram package only supports diagrams of order four, which produces 16 areas, including the empty set.

Fig. 5.1 Venn diagram of three necessity relations in mvQCA

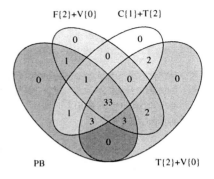

```
> library("VennDiagram")
> vennHarKemNec <- venn.diagram(
+   x = list(
+     "PB" = which(HarKem$PB == 1),
+     "T{2}+V{0}" = which(COms[ , 1] == 1),
+     "F{2}+V{0}" = which(COms[ , 2] == 1),
+     "C{1}+T{2}" = which(COms[ , 3] == 1)),
+   filename = NULL,
+   cex = 2.5, cat.cex = 2, cat.pos = c(180, 180, 0, 0),
+   cat.dist = c(0.4, 0.4, 0.12, 0.12),
+   fill = gray(c(0.3, 0.5, 0.7, 0.9))
+ )
> grid.draw(vennHarKemNec)
```

The resulting Venn diagram is shown in Fig. 5.1.

5.1.2 Analyzing Sufficiency Relations

Analogous to necessity inclusion, sufficiency inclusion of some condition level $\mathbf{C}\{v_l\}$, $\text{Incl}_S(\mathbf{C}\{v_l\})$, is computed as given by Eq. (5.3).

$$\text{Incl}_S(\mathbf{C}\{v_l\}) = \frac{\sum_{i=1}^{n} o_i = 1 | \{v_l\}\, c_i = 1}{\sum_{i=1}^{n} \{v_l\}\, c_i = 1} \tag{5.3}$$

Accordingly, the formula for sufficiency coverage $\text{Cov}_S(\mathbf{C}\{v_l\})$ is given by Eq. (5.4).

$$\text{Cov}_S(\mathbf{C}\{v_l\}) = \frac{\sum_{i=1}^{n} o_i = 1 | \{v_l\}\, c_i = 1}{\sum_{i=1}^{n} o_i = 1} \tag{5.4}$$

The construction of truth tables for csQCA and fsQCA is achieved with the truthTable() function, which works likewise for mvQCA.

```
> HarKemTT <- truthTable(HarKem, outcome = "PB",
+  conditions = c("C", "F", "T", "V"), incl.cut0 = 0.4,
+  show.cases = TRUE, sort.by = c("incl","n"))
> HarKemTT

      C F T V  OUT n  incl  PRI    cases
35    1 2 2 0   1  7  1.000 1.000  BF,TD,KM,DJ,GA,GN,MR
17    0 2 2 0   1  6  1.000 1.000  CV,GQ,ER,GW,LR,SO
29    1 1 2 0   1  4  1.000 1.000  CF,CM,CI,TG
..    . . . .   .  .  ..... ..... ...........
<<rest omitted>>
```

In order to replicate the truth table from Hartmann and Kammerzell (2010) and code configuration $C\{2\} \cdot F\{1\} \cdot T\{2\} \cdot V\{1\}$ as a contradiction, the argument incl.cut0 has to be used. All non-remainder configurations with inclusion scores between incl.cut0 and incl.cut1 are coded as contradictions.

Hartmann and Kammerzell (2010) present the parsimonious solution, which can be generated using the eqmcc() function with the same arguments that were also used for csQCA in Sect. 3.3.4.1 and fsQCA in Sect. 4.3.4.1.

```
> HarKemSP <- eqmcc(HarKemTT, include = "?", details = TRUE)
> HarKemSP

n OUT = 1/0/C: 40/4/4
  Total      : 48

S1: C{0} + C{1} + F{2} + T{1}*V{0} + T{2}*V{0}

                 incl    PRI    cov.r  cov.u
-------------------------------------------------
1  C{0}          1.000  1.000  0.333  0.024
2  C{1}          1.000  1.000  0.405  0.048
3  F{2}          1.000  1.000  0.619  0.048
4  T{1}*V{0}     1.000  1.000  0.143  0.048
5  T{2}*V{0}     1.000  1.000  0.571  0.048
-------------------------------------------------
   S1            1.000  1.000  0.952
```

The minimization yields one minimal sum consisting of five PIs. However, the study by Hartmann and Kemmerzell provides a prime example for the all.sol argument of the eqmcc() function.[3] Current QCA practice only focuses on those minimal sums with the least number of PIs in deriving the solution. However, there

---

[3] This argument has been suggested by Michael Baumgartner.

may exist PIs with more literals than the most efficient path, or minimal sums with more PIs than the minimal number, or both.

```
> eqmcc(HarKemTT, include = "?", all.sol = TRUE, rowdom = FALSE)

S1: C{0} + C{1} + F{2} + T{1}*V{0} + (T{2}*V{0})
S2: C{0} + C{1} + F{2} + T{1}*V{0} + (F{0}*T{2} + F{1}*V{0})
```

Minimal sum S_1 consists of five, but S_2 of six PIs. However, $\mathbf{T}\{2\} \cdot \mathbf{V}\{0\}$ implies the same configurations as $\mathbf{F}\{0\} \cdot \mathbf{T}\{2\} + \mathbf{F}\{1\} \cdot \mathbf{V}\{0\}$ and both fit the data equally well. This phenomenon requires a separate theoretical treatment and will not be further analyzed herein. In the remainder of this chapter, we will therefore concentrate of S_1.

Factorization and collapsing simplify S_1 to three terms, and the entire solution can again be visualized in a Venn diagram with VennDiagram's venn.diagram() function. Similar to the coms component in objects returned by superSubset(), eqmcc() returns a pims component, which contains all <u>PI</u> <u>m</u>embership <u>s</u>cores. As it is the <u>p</u>arsimonious <u>sol</u>ution for which these scores are required, the relevant subcomponent of pims is p.sol.

```
> (PIms <- HarKemSP$pims$p.sol)

    C{0} C{1} F{2} T{1}*V{0} T{2}*V{0}
AO    1    0    1       0          0
BJ    0    1    1       1          0
BW    0    0    0       0          0
..    .    .    .       .          .
<<rest omitted>>
```

When the PIms data frame is now combined with the usual application of the which() function to produce an auxiliary incidence table, the plot in Fig. 5.2 results.

```
> vennHarKemSuf <- venn.diagram(
+  x = list(
+    "PB" = which(HarKem$PB == 1),
+    "C{0,1}" = which((PIms[,1] | PIms[,2]) == 1),
+    "F{2}" = which(PIms[,3] == 1),
+    "T{1,2}*V{0}" = which((PIms[,4] | PIms[,5]) == 1)),
+  filename = NULL,
+  cex = 2.5, cat.cex = 2, cat.pos = c(180, 180, 0, 0),
+  cat.dist = c(0.4, 0.4, 0.12, 0.12),
+  fill = gray(c(0.3, 0.5, 0.7, 0.9))
+ )
> grid.draw(vennHarKemSuf)
```

Fig. 5.2 Venn diagram of parsimonious solution PIs in mvQCA

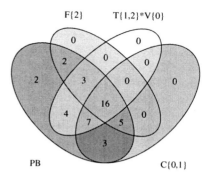

The structure of this code is very similar to that used for producing Fig. 5.1. Additional code only has to be added for those conditions where more than one category either represents an individual PI as in **C** {0, 1}, or appears in conjunction with an identical category of another condition as in **T** {0, 1} · **V** {0}.

The QCA package is the first software to offer intermediate solutions for mvQCA. In the current framework of mvQCA, value labels denote full membership in one of at least three mutually exclusive set categories. Directional expectations for multi-value crisp sets require the specification of these labels, separated by semicolons and enclosed by double quotes if more than one category is to be specified. The provision of a value indicates that the presence of this category is expected to contribute to an outcome value of "1", while implicitly, QCA assumes that it is the absence of all remaining categories. For example, if having a French colonial background, no or only limited regime type competition, a managed mode of transition and ethnic violence are individually expected to contribute to a subset-relation between each configuration in which these categories are contained and the provision of party bans, the following specification should be used in the argument for <u>directional</u> expectations direxp.

```
> HarKemSI <- eqmcc(HarKemTT, include = "?",
+  direxp = c(1,"1;2",2,1), details = TRUE)
> HarKemSI

n OUT = 1/0/C: 40/4/4
  Total     : 48

p.sol: C{0} + C{1} + F{2} + T{1}*V{0} + T{2}*V{0}

S1:   C{1} + F{2} + T{1}*V{0} + T{2}*V{0} + C{0}*F{1}*T{2}
```

		incl	PRI	cov.r	cov.u
1	C{1}	1.000	1.000	0.405	0.048
2	F{2}	1.000	1.000	0.619	0.143
3	T{1}*V{0}	1.000	1.000	0.143	0.048
4	T{2}*V{0}	1.000	1.000	0.571	0.048
5	C{0}*F{1}*T{2}	1.000	1.000	0.071	0.024
	S1	1.000	1.000	0.952	

Both the intermediate solution and the parsimonious solution from which it has been derived are printed.

5.2 Temporal QCA

Despite its roots in historical sociology, the incorporation of temporal sequences in QCA has only recently become a topic of discussion in the literature (Caren and Panofsky 2005; Ragin and Strand 2008), although a suitable procedure had already been suggested by Ragin (1987, p. 162). A QCA involving information about the sequencing of events is known as temporal QCA (tQCA). In tQCA, the set of conditions usually consists of the set of substantive conditions, and a set of auxiliary conditions which describe sequential pairings among the substantive conditions. With k_s substantive conditions, there can be up to $k_a = (k_s^2 - k_s)/2$ auxiliary conditions. However, not all of the 2^{k_a} configurations are transitive and need to be included in the full truth table. More precisely, only $k_s!$ configurations are transitive and therefore potentially plausible. For example, with three substantive conditions C_1, C_2 and C_3, there are $k_a = (k_s^2 - k_s)/2 = 3$ auxiliary conditions $C_{1/2}$, $C_{1/3}$ and $C_{2/3}$ that together form $k_s! = 6$ transitive configurations.

We use the hypothetical dataset of 18 cases of unionization attempts by graduate student workers at research universities introduced in Caren and Panofsky (2005) and re-analyzed in Ragin and Strand (2008).[4] The conditions indicate whether the university is public (**P**: 1-yes, 0-no), elite allies have been present (**E**: 1-yes, 0-no), the university has been affiliated with a national union (**A**: 1-yes, 0-no) and whether a strike or strike threat has been present (**S**: 1-yes, 0-no). The outcome indicates whether the union has been recognized or not (**REC**: 1-yes, 0-no), and a fifth, auxiliary condition whether elite allies had been present before the university has become affiliated with a national union or not (**EBA**: 1-yes, 0-no).

When either of the two events **E** and **A** did not occur, it is impossible to establish a sequence.[5] These combinations are usually coded as "don't care" and are ignored

---

[4] Only the set names have been changed.

[5] Sometimes the non-occurrence of an event may play a role so that event sequences could be established for events that did not happen. In this example, however, we simply replicate the analysis.

during minimization. QCA indicators for a "don't care" value in auxiliary conditions can be a dash ("-"), the value "dc" or any negative integer.[6]

```
> data(RagStr)
> RagStr

  P E A S EBA REC
1 1 1 1 1   1   1
2 1 1 1 1   1   1
3 1 1 1 1   0   1
. . . . .   .   .
<<rest omitted>>
```

As usual, the truth table can be constructed with the truthTable() function. Note that QCA also automatically takes care of the auxiliary condition **EBA**. Conditions which contain any of the accepted indicators for a "don't care" value are always excluded from the computation of parameters of fit.

```
> RagStrTT <- truthTable(RagStr, outcome = "REC")
```

The minimization is again performed by eqmcc().

```
> eqmcc(RagStrTT, details = TRUE, show.cases = TRUE)

n OUT = 1/0/C: 7/10/0
  Total      : 17

Number of multiple-covered cases: 3

S1: P*E*S + E*A*S*eba + P*E*A*EBA
```

		incl	PRI	cov.r	cov.u	cases
1	P*E*S	1.000	1.000	0.571	0.143	6; 3; 1,2
2	E*A*S*eba	1.000	1.000	0.571	0.143	13; 3
3	P*E*A*EBA	1.000	1.000	0.714	0.286	4,5; 1,2
	S1	1.000	1.000	1.000		

The minimal sum consists of all substantive as well as both literals of the auxiliary condition **EBA**. This solution can be written more efficiently by eliminating **EBA** again after having transposed the information it contained into sequence notation using the forward slash "/" as the temporal separator.

$$P/E/S + A/E/S + P/E/A \rightarrow REC$$

---

[6] This flexibility allows to directly import datasets that have been initially prepared for fs/QCA, which uses a dash, and QCA3, which uses the value "-9".

Substantively, this formula translates into three statements. Graduate student unions are recognized when graduate students at a public university have had the support of elite allies and then threatened to strike, or when graduate students (irrespective of whether the university was public) have become affiliated with a national union, then gained elite allies and finally threatened to strike, or when graduate students at a public university have had the support of elite allies before they became affiliated with a union.

References

Abell P (1990) Supporting industrial cooperatives in developing countries: some Tanzanian experiences. Econ Ind Democr 11(4):483–504

Amenta E, Carruthers BG, Zylan Y (1992) A hero for the aged: the townsend movement, the political mediation model, and United-States old-age policy, 1934–1950. Am J Sociol 98(2):308–339

Arfi B (2010) Linguistic fuzzy logic methods in social sciences. Springer, Berlin

Arvind TT, Stirton L (2010) Explaining the reception of the code Napoleon in Germany: a fuzzy-set qualitative comparative analysis. Legal Stud 30(1):1–29

Avdagic S (2010) When are concerted reforms feasible? explaining the emergence of social pacts in Western Europe. Comp Polit Stud 43(5):628–657

Bakker RM, Cambre B, Korlaar L, Raab J (2011) Managing the project learning paradox: a set-theoretic approach toward project knowledge transfer. Int J Project Manag 29(5):494–503

Blackman T (2008) Can smoking cessation services be better targeted to tackle health inequalities? Evidence from a cross-sectional study. Health Educ J 67(2):91–101

Bojadziev G, Bojadziev M (2007) Fuzzy logic for business, finance, and management, 2nd edn. World Scientific, New Jersey

Boudet HS, Jayasundera DC, Davis J (2011) Drivers of conflict in developing country infrastructure projects: experience from the water and pipeline sectors. J Constr Eng Manag 137(7):498–511

Caren N, Panofsky A (2005) TQCA: a technique for adding temporality to qualitative comparative analysis. Sociol Methods Res 34(2):147–172

Chambers JM (2008) Software for data analysis: programming with R. Springer, New York

Chan S (2003) Explaining war termination: a Boolean analysis of causes. J Peace Res 40(1):49–66

Chen H (2012) VennDiagram: generate high-resolution Venn and Euler plots. R package version 1.1.3

Chen H, Boutros P (2011) VennDiagram: a package for the generation of highly-customizable Venn and Euler diagrams in R. BMC Bioinformatics 12(1):35–41

Clark TD, Larson JM, Mordeson JN, Potter JD, Wierman MJ (2008) Applying fuzzy mathematics to formal models in comparative politics. Springer, Berlin

Cooper B, Glaesser J (2011) Paradoxes and pitfalls in using fuzzy set QCA: illustrations from a critical review of a study of educational inequality. Sociol Res Online 16(3):8

Coppedge M, Gerring J, Altman D, Bernhard M, Fish S, Hicken A, Kroenig M, Lindberg SI, McMann K, Paxton P, Semetko HA, Skaaning SE, Staton J, Teorell J (2011) Conceptualizing and measuring democracy: a new approach. Perspect Polit 9(2):247–267

Coverdill JE, Finlay W, Martin JK (1994) Labor management in the Southern textile industry. Sociol Methods Res 23(1):54–85

Cronqvist L (2011) Tosmana—tool for small-n analysis, Version 1.3.2. University of Trier, Trier

Cronqvist L, Berg-Schlosser D (2009) Multi-value QCA (mvQCA). In: Rihoux B, Ragin CC (eds) Configurational comparative methods: qualitative comparative analysis (QCA) and related techniques. Sage, London, pp 69–86

Downey J, Stanyer J (2010) Comparative media analysis: why some fuzzy thinking might help. Applying fuzzy set qualitative comparative analysis to the personalization of mediated political communication. Eur J Commun 25(4):331–347

Dușa A (2007a) Enhancing Quine-McCluskey (WP 2007-49). COMPASSS. Available from: http://www.compasss.org

Dușa A (2007b) User manual for the QCA(GUI) package in R. J Bus Res 60(5):576–586

Dușa A (2010) A mathematical approach to the Boolean minimization problem. Qual Quant 44(1):99–113

Emmenegger P (2011) Job security regulations in Western democracies: a fuzzy set analysis. Eur J Polit Res 50(3):336–364

Evans AJ, Aligica PD (2008) The spread of the flat tax in Eastern Europe. East Eur Econ 46(3):49–67

Freitag M, Schlicht R (2009) Educational federalism in Germany: foundations of social inequality in education. Governance 22(1):47–72

Glaesser J, Cooper B (2011) Selectivity and flexibility in the German secondary school system: a configurational analysis of recent data from the German socio-economic panel. Eur Sociol Rev 27(5):570–585

Goertz G (2006) Social science concepts: a user's guide. Princeton University Press, Princeton

Greckhamer T (2011) Cross-cultural differences in compensation level and inequality across occupations: a set-theoretic analysis. Organ Stud 32(1):85–115

Greckhamer T, Misangyi VF, Elms H, Lacey R (2008) Using qualitative comparative analysis in strategic management research. Organ Res Methods 11(4):695–726

Griffin LJ, Botsko C, Wahl AM, Isaac LW (1991) Theoretical generality, case particularity—qualitative comparative analysis of trade-union growth and decline. Int J Comp Sociol 32(1–2):110–136

Harkreader S, Imershein AW (1999) The conditions for state action in Florida's health-care market. J Health Soc Behav 40(2):159–174

Hartmann C, Kemmerzell J (2010) Understanding variations in party bans in Africa. Democratization 17(4):642–665

Hellström E (1998) Qualitative comparative analysis: a useful tool for research into forest policy and forestry conflicts. For Sci 44(2):254–265

Hollingsworth R, Hanneman R, Hage J, Ragin C (1996) The effect of human capital and state intervention on the performance of medical systems. Soc Forces 75(2):459–484

Huang R (2012) QCA3: yet another package for qualitative comparative analysis. R package version 0.0-5

Kaeding M (2008) Necessary conditions for the effective transposition of EU legislation. Policy Polit 36(2):261–281

Kitchener M, Beynon M, Harrington C (2002) Qualitative comparative analysis and public services research: lessons from an early application. Public Manag Rev 4(4):485–504

Koenig-Archibugi M (2004) Explaining government preferences for institutional change in EU foreign and security policy. Int Organ 58(1):137–174

Krook ML (2010) Women's representation in parliament: a qualitative comparative analysis. Polit Stud 58(5):886–908

Kvist J (2006) Diversity, ideal types and fuzzy sets in comparative welfare state research. In: Rihoux B, Grimm H (eds) Innovative comparative methods for policy analysis, Springer, New York, pp 167–184

Longest KC, Vaisey S (2008) fuzzy: a program for performing qualitative comparative analyses (QCA) in Stata. Stata J 8(1):79–104

Maat Evd (2011) Sleeping hegemons: third-party intervention following territorial integrity transgressions. J Peace Res 48(2):201–215

Maggetti M (2007) De facto independence after delegation: a fuzzy-set analysis. Regul Gov 1(4):271–294

Miethe TD, Drass KA (1999) Exploring the social context of instrumental and expressive homicides: an application of qualitative comparative analysis. J Quant Crim 15(1):1–21

Moritz M, Giblin J, Ciccone M, Davis A, Fuhrman J, Kimiaie M, Madzsar S, Olson K, Senn M (2011) Social risk-management strategies in pastoral systems: a qualitative comparative analysis. Cross-Cult Res 45(3):286–317

Munck GL, Verkuilen J (2002) Conceptualizing and measuring democracy: evaluating alternative indices. Comp Polit Stud 35(1):5–34

Musheno MC, Gregware PR, Drass KA (1991) Court management of AIDS disputes: a sociolegal analysis. Law Soc Inquiry 16(4):737–774

Oldekop JA, Bebbington AJ, Brockington DAN, Preziosi RF (2010) Understanding the lessons and limitations of conservation and development. Conserv Biol 24(2):461–469

Pennings P (2003) Beyond dichotomous explanations: explaining constitutional control of the executive with fuzzy-sets. Eur J Polit Res 42(4):541–567

Ragin C (1989) The logic of the comparative method and the algebra of logic. J Quant Anthropol 1(4):373–398

Ragin C (1999) Using qualitative comparative analysis to study causal complexity. Health Serv Res 34(5, Part 2):1225–1239

Ragin CC (1987) The comparative method: moving beyond qualitative and quantative strategies. University of California Press, Berkeley

Ragin CC (2000) Fuzzy-set social science. University of Chicago Press, Chicago

Ragin CC (2008) Redesigning social inquiry: fuzzy sets and beyond. University of Chicago Press, Chicago

Ragin CC (2009) Qualitative comparative analysis using fuzzy sets (fsQCA). In: Rihoux B, Ragin CC (eds) Configurational comparative methods: qualitative comparative analysis (QCA) and related techniques, Sage, London, pp 87–121

Ragin CC, Davey S (2009) fs/QCA: fuzzy-set/qualitative comparative analysis [version 2.5]. Department of Sociology. University of Arizona, Tucson

Ragin CC, Strand SI (2008) Using qualitative comparative analysis to study causal order: comment on Caren and Panofsky (2005). Sociol Methods Res 36(4):431–441

Ragin CC, Mayer SE, Drass KA (1984) Assessing discrimination: a Boolean approach. Am Sociol Rev 49(2):221–234

Rihoux B, Ragin CC (eds) (2009) Configurational comparative methods: qualitative comparative analysis (QCA) and related techniques. Sage, London

Romme AGL (1995) Self-organizing processes in top management teams: a Boolean comparative approach. J Bus Res 34(1):11–34

Rudel T, Roper J (1996) Regional patterns and historical trends in tropical deforestation, 1976–1990: a qualitative comparative analysis. Ambio 25(3):160–166

Schensul J, Chandran D, Singh S, Berg M, Singh S, Gupta K (2010) The use of qualitative comparative analysis for critical event research in alcohol and HIV in Mumbai, India. AIDS Behav 14(S1):113–125

Schneider CQ, Wagemann C (2012) Set-theoretic methods for the social sciences: a guide to qualitative comparative analysis (QCA). Cambridge University Press, Cambridge

Schneider MR, Schulze-Bentrop C, Paunescu M (2010) Mapping the institutional capital of high-tech firms: a fuzzy-set analysis of capitalist variety and export performance. J Int Bus Stud 41(2):246–266

Schneider P, Sadowski D (2010) The impact of new public management instruments on PhD education. Higher Educ 59(5):543–565

Scouvart M, Adams RT, Caldas M, Dale V, Mertens B, Nedelec V, Pacheco P, Rihoux B, Lambin EF (2008) Causes of deforestation in the Brazilian Amazon: a qualitative comparative analysis. J Land Use Sci 2(4):257–282

Sebastian R, Parameswaran A (2007) Conversion and the family: Chinese Hare Krishnas. J Contemp Religion 22(3):341–359

Stevenson WB, Greenberg D (2000) Agency and social networks: strategies of action in a social structure of position, opposition, and opportunity. Adm Sci Q 45(4):651–678

Stokke OS (2007) Qualitative comparative analysis, shaming, and international regime effectiveness. J Bus Res 60(5):501–511

Thiem A (2010) Set-relational fit and the formulation of transformational rules in fsQCA (WP 2010-61). COMPASSS. Available from: http://www.compasss.org

Thiem A (2011) Conditions of intergovernmental armaments cooperation in Western Europe, 1996–2006. Eur Polit Sci Rev 3(1):1–33

Vaisey S (2009) QCA 3.0: The "Ragin Revolution" continues. Contemp Sociol J Rev 38(4):308–312

Valliere D, Na N, Wise S (2008) Prior relationships and M&A exit valuations: a set-theoretic approach. J Private Equity 11(2):60–72

Verkuilen J (2005) Assigning membership in a fuzzy set analysis. Sociol Methods Res 33(4):462–496

Vis B (2009) Governments and unpopular social policy reform: biting the bullet or steering clear? Eur J Polit Res 48(1):31–57

Werner T (2009) Congressmen of the silent South: the persistence of Southern racial liberals, 1949–1964. J Polit 71(1):70–81

Wickham-Crowley TP (1991) A qualitative comparative approach to Latin American revolutions. Int J Comp Sociol 32(1–2):82–109

Williams LM, Farrell RA (1990) Legal response to child sexual abuse in day care. Crim Justice Behav 17(3):284–302

Woodside AG, Hsu SY, Marshall R (2011) General theory of cultures' consequences on international tourism behavior. J Bus Res 64(8):785–799

Zuur AF, Ieno EN, Meesters E (2009) A beginner's guide to R. Springer, New York

Index

A
abline(), 67, 81
Access, 23
as.integer(), 16

B
Bar chart, 29– 31
barplot(), 29, 30
Base variable, 27, 31, 51–55,
    57, 58, 60, 61

C
c(), 11, 12, 16, 40
calibrate(), 31, 58, 59, 60
Calibration, 51
    direct assignment, 51, 54
    direct method, 55
    external criteria, 27
    fuzzification, 51, 53, 61
    internal criteria, 27
    transformational assignment, 51, 55
cbind(), 13
Cluster analysis, 29, 31
Complex solution. *See* solution type
Concept type, 52
    end-point, 52, 53, 55, 56, 59
    mid-point, 52, 53, 56, 57, 59
Concept type relation, 52
Configuration
    true, 39, 40, 70, 71
    false, 39, 40, 70

Logical remainder, 41, 42, 44–48,
    71, 73
Counterfactual, 41, 72
createMatrix(), 22
Cronqvist, Lasse, 83

D
Data frame. *See* Data structure
Data structure
    data frame, 14
    list, 14, 19
    matrix, 13
    vector, 12
Data type
    character, 15, 16
    double, 15, 16
    integer, 15
    logical, 15
    numeric, 15, 16
data(), 62
data.frame(), 14, 28
Density plot, 30, 31
density(), 31
Directional expectation, 44, 45, 75, 76, 89

E
edit(), 17
End-point concept. *See* concept type
eqmcc(), 40–43, 46, 47, 49, 71–79,
    87, 88, 91
Excel, 23

A. Thiem and A. Duşa, *Qualitative Comparative Analysis with R*,
SpringerBriefs in Political Science, DOI: 10.1007/978-1-4614-4584-5,
© The Author(s) 2013

CPSIA information can be obtained at www.ICGtesting.com
Printed in the USA
LVOW10s1804090714

393589LV00008B/285/P